THE
MACHIAVELLIAN'S
GUIDE
TO
Insults

THE MACHIAVELLIAN'S GUIDE TO
Insults

Nick Casanova

iUniverse, Inc.

New York   Bloomington   Shanghai

The Machiavellian's Guide to Insults

iUniverse books may be ordered through booksellers or by contacting:

iUniverse
1663 Liberty Drive
Bloomington, IN 47403
www.iuniverse.com
1-800-Authors (1-800-288-4677)

Because of the dynamic nature of the Internet, any Web addresses or links contained in this book may have changed since publication and may no longer be valid.

The views expressed in this work are solely those of the author and do not necessarily reflect the views of the publisher, and the publisher hereby disclaims any responsibility for them.

ISBN: 978-0-595-48729-5 (pbk)
ISBN: 978-0-595-48876-6 (cloth)
ISBN: 978-0-595-60824-9 (ebk)

Printed in the United States of America

For my brother Paul, who is far too diplomatic to say any of the things suggested herein

Contents

Part II   Appearances

Part III   Sex and Sexuality

Part IV   Personality Types

Part V   Vices and Other Weaknesses

Part VI   The Ham-Handed Compliment/Insult

Part VII Be Annoying

Introduction

How often have you been faced with a confrontation where the best response you could come up with was to swear? Unfortunately, such words say more about you than your enemy. Far better to calmly wound him with a tailor-made barb aimed at one of his weaknesses, without coming across as if you've been affected yourself. It is often said that nobody wins a verbal fight, but this isn't true: the winner is simply the one who sustains the least damage while inflicting the most.

Often, the best putdown is the one that seems on the surface to be well-intentioned. Ham-handed attempts to relate or sympathize can be the most effective ways of underlining your opponent's weaknesses. These are far more humiliating than any angry outburst could ever be. Insults, like flattery, work best when seemingly unintended. And if you act under the guise of friendliness, it makes it harder for your victim to retaliate. You can always, of course, be overtly antagonistic—but there's no need to be. This book suggests a range of behaviors, from the subtle putdown to the outright declaration of war.

All of this begs the question of why you would want to insult anyone. There are two sections of this book, *Deflating Big Egos* and *Personality Types*, which describe the kinds of people who deserve to be insulted: those with narcissistic personalities. The other sections mostly describe weaknesses—such as appearance—which can be used as leverage in any war of words. Nobody deserves to be savaged on the basis of his appearance, but if you are at war with your opponent because of his low character, his appearance—or his vices, or his love life—can all provide handy vehicles through which to reach him. If your victim is human (i.e., tall or short, skinny or fat, rich or poor), you will find ammunition here. In any case, you undoubtedly have your own reasons for wanting to insult somebody, not least of which is that he has insulted you.

Niccolo Machiavelli, had he written a book on insults, would have told you to make sure they suited your opponent, to deliver them without a trace of anger in your voice. If you are obviously angry when you deliver an insult, your enemy will just ascribe it to your anger, and write it off. But if you deliver it in a calm, detached way, it will sting much more.

Those to whom cattiness comes naturally do not need this book. But for those of you who sit and stew over a slight because you couldn't think of the appropriate rejoinder at the moment, here are some weapons for your arsenal, to have ready at the appropriate moment. People often quote the old cliché about how revenge is a dish best served cold; in fact, it tastes best piping hot.

The book will generally use the masculine gender, but this is simply a matter of form. And it will refer to your opponent as "your victim"—because that is what he will be if you follow the instructions herein.

PART I
Deflating Big Egos

The Proud Owner
of a New Car

There's nothing that proclaims our status—or our values—quite so immediately as a car, which is why so many people put so much stock in them. In our society, in a sense, you *are* your car. So when your victim proudly shows off his new automobile, this is a wonderful opportunity to put him down.

Your first response should be, "You like that color?" He will say, "Yeah, don't you?" If it's an uncommon shade, respond, "Well, it's not a very popular color, that's all." If it's common, respond, "It's just that it's the same color everybody else is getting these days."

If your victim's car is foreign, say, "I'm patriotic enough to want to buy a car made in the U.S.A. Call me foolish, but that's just the way I am." This should put him on the defensive. If your victim's car is domestic, ask, "Aren't foreign cars supposed to be better built?"

If your victim's car is big, ask, "What kind of gas mileage does this thing get?"

Ask your victim if the car has an alarm system. If it doesn't, say, "I hear this is one of the most popular models with the chop shops."

If your victim fancies himself a member of the intelligentsia, ask, "Isn't this the kind of car you normally see with a pair of Styrofoam dice hanging from the rearview mirror and a stencil of a naked girl on the side?"

Ask how much he paid for the car. Then say, "Thirty-five thousand! I have a friend who got this exact same car for thirty." After your victim explains that this is the model with leather seats and a V-6, say,

"Yeah, he got those too." Shake your head and mutter, "These dealers are such rip-off artists."

If it's a cheap car, nod judiciously and say, "I guess there's no point to wasting money on a fancy car. An econobox makes much more sense on your budget."

If it's an expensive car, take a different tack. After he lovingly demonstrates the sound system that holds six CDs, the mist control, the navigation system, the automatically dimming rearview mirror, and the retractable moon roof, just shrug and say, "To me, a car is a just a way to get from point A to point B. I never felt I needed a car to affirm my identity."

At this point, your victim will bridle and say something to the effect that he doesn't either. Interrupt him: "No, no, you don't understand—all I'm saying is that I feel like a complete person without one."

Conclude, "Well, congratulations, I guess. You're now a prime target for a carjacker."

The Proud Homeowner

Some people are just a bit too proud of their houses. They actually think that their home is their castle—literally. If your victim suffers from this delusion, and ever gives you a tour of his castle, have some appropriate comments ready.

If he informs you that the countertops are Corian, ask, "Does that make the food taste better?" If he points out that the faucets are gold-plated, ask, "Does that make the water purer?"

The all-purpose response to any such point on the tour is, "So what?"

Ask about termites. After your victim says he's already had somebody in to check for them, tell him, "Believe me, those guys don't always know what they're doing. Termites love a house like this. Look over there at that crack in the wall. That might be termites."

Or, "This whole area is high in radon because of all the bedrock."

"Is the groundwater in this area still contaminated, or have they cleaned that up?"

Ask your victim how much each of the furnishings cost.

If you see a nice leather sofa, comment, "It's amazing how they can make Naugahyde look almost like leather these days."

If you see dust, run your finger along wherever it has accumulated, then look at your finger with raised eyebrows. If there's enough of it, write "Clean me" in it.

If any paint is peeling, point out, "I think you need a new coat over here."

If your victim is a Martha Stewart wannabe, and takes pride in her ability to put the various elements of the house together, say, "It always kills me when people think they're being 'creative' by buying stuff for their house. If they were so creative, they'd write a book or paint a picture. What kind of creativity does it take to go shopping, for Crissakes?"

If your victim wants you to be impressed by the size of his house, oblige him: "Wow, this is a real white elephant! What's the upkeep on a place like this?" After he replies, comment, "Mark my words, you're going to be a slave to this place. Cleaning, vacuuming, mowing the lawn. Ugh."

Ask, "What did you pay for this place, two forty?" (Underestimate by 40 percent.)

If it's a small house, it's even easier to put your victim on the defensive. Say appreciatively, "This is a nice, unpretentious house." (That's real estate lingo for "small and inexpensive.")

"This is a nice, cozy, little bungalow." A bungalow, of course, is the next thing to a shack, which is the next thing to a corrugated tin roof shanty.

"I swear, this place has the exact same floor plan as the little guest cottage at my parents' house. They bought it prefab."

When you step outside to see the grounds, look back at the house, then smack your forehead as if you've just had an epiphany. "I knew I'd seen this house somewhere before!" When your victim asks where, reply, "On the highway, on one of those trucks marked 'wide load.' Wow—I actually saw it when it was being delivered!"

Ask, "Isn't this what's known in real estate lingo as a 'teardown'?"

If his property is small, say, "Personally, I'd rather commute an extra ten miles than have to live on a lot the size of a postage stamp."

If the house next door is bigger, you can say, "You know, from a distance, it sort of looks like that's the manor and this is the detached garage." Quickly add, "You know, a four-car garage."

If you want to declare war, say, "You know how some houses are converted barns? This must be a converted outhouse."

If you do all this, you'll cure your victim of his habit of giving house tours. If you do it really well, the house should be on the market in the near future.

Rich Man

In our society, a tall, handsome, brilliant, charming teacher with a killer sense of humor is considered less successful than a short, fat, ugly, dumb, obnoxious investment banker. It may not be fair, but that's the way it is. If your victim is that investment banker, it is up to you to make sure he understands the ridiculousness of the situation.

You can't attack him *because* he's rich; but rich people do have their own money-derived set of insecurities.

If your victim has inherited his money, he's easy pickings. Heirs generally don't flaunt their wealth and tend to be very insecure about whether people like them for their money. Don't drive this point home by pointing out that his relationships are all based on his wealth. Drive it home by saying the opposite: "You know, you're a nice guy. I don't just like you for your money, you know." You'll have made your point. (People generally don't take the trouble to voluntarily deny something unless it's true.)

If your victim has a good-looking wife, say, "Sally seems like a nice woman. She doesn't come across like a gold-digger at all." Sound slightly surprised as you say this, as if you had expected the opposite. Your victim will probably say that she isn't a gold-digger. Reply, "Oh, no, of course not." Add, "When she married you, she *did* say 'for richer or poorer,' right?" Then let a little smirk slip through.

If he's inherited wealth, but doesn't know that you know it, ask, in reference to another heir, "How come people who inherit money are always so screwed up?"

If your victim is self-made, he is far more likely to flaunt his wealth. When he shows you his new helicopter pad, instead of acting impressed, just shake your head and say, "It's easier for a camel to fit through the eye of a needle than for a rich man to ascend to the kingdom of heaven."

If he still works, point out, "There's only one way to say you're rich that really counts." When he asks what that is, reply, "Wanna go fishing Wednesday?"

Then ask, "What are you so insecure about? What is it you're trying to compensate for?"

"Does your money make you feel six feet tall?" (Substitute whatever is appropriate here: young, handsome, etc.)

Add, "Too bad you can't buy people's respect."

Ask your victim what the threshold is for being considered "rich." He will then probably ask you the same question (rich people are always concerned with this). Simply set the threshold above his level. If he has one million, say five. If he has five, say ten. And so on.

If your victim takes a dim view of any of your comments, and gets angry, respond, "Look at you ... I guess money doesn't buy happiness after all."

Poor Man

In our country, with so much emphasis on money, a poor person will almost always have at least a little chip on his shoulder. If you're rich yourself, it's a relatively easy matter to set that chip aflame.

When you're with your poor victim, always refer to success in purely monetary terms. ("He's done quite well for himself; he's worth at least five million dollars.") Always refer to people's "worth," as if a human being's innate worth is measured in dollars and cents.

Refer to other rich people as "quality people," or, if you're from the South, "quality folks." Never refer to poor people this way; soon enough, it will become apparent what gives these folks their "quality."

Or, talk about how a rich friend comes from a "good family." (Only refer to rich families this way.)

If your victim talks about how we have to help the downtrodden, shrug and say, "Let them eat cake," and let out a hearty laugh. Refer to the poor as the "common people," "hoi polloi," the "great unwashed," and "peasants."

If your victim is of a leftist bent and suggests that the poor should be up in arms about their lot, reply, "Yep, they're revolting all right." If he doesn't catch your drift, add, "In both senses of the term."

Upon seeing some obviously insane or drug-addicted homeless person in the street, point out, "That's what happens when you don't do your homework."

Suggest that the income tax be abolished.

Refer to a middle-class couple you know as being "poor as church mice. They don't have two nickels to rub together." Drip contempt as you say this, as if they are exhibiting incredible gall for being that way.

Laugh and say, "You know that guy in the Lotto ads, the one in his pool with that float? That's me." But then discount the role that luck played: "I guess society views me as being worth a quarter of a million a year," as if a large number of reasonable people had come to this balanced judgment. Add, without a scintilla of self-doubt, "But I tell you what, I'm worth every penny. They get good value for that money."

If your victim tells you about a good purchase he made, reply, "You shop at Costco? Why?" After your victim explains that he does it to save money, act taken aback and say, "Oh," in a tone that makes clear this is a novel concept.

Conclude by being falsely philosophical: "Ah, money's not that important." Gesture expansively. "Do my Mercedes, my mansion make me happy? Of course not. I get my meaning in life from my family, my friends, my work." After everything else you've said, reciting this trite cliché will ring totally false.

At some point, your victim will lash back. Respond, "What are you talking about? I could buy and sell you ten times over and not miss the difference," as if this settles any and all arguments. If your victim points out that he's not for sale, reply, "Don't be silly. We all have our price ... It's just that mine is a little higher than yours, that's all."

Talk about Your Wealthy Friend

If your victim is poor—not one of the happy poor, but one of the disgruntled poor—one way to rub his face in his poverty is to talk about your rich friend and his sybaritic lifestyle. Show no signs of jealousy as you talk about your friend's fabulous wealth; this will make your victim all the more jealous.

This friend needn't actually exist; just invent him and tell your victim about him. Claim that your imaginary friend, let's call him Bill, made all his money in the stock market. Since your victim probably hasn't done all that well in the market, the thought of Bill's luck (it's always luck when somebody else does better than you) will gall. If your victim asks how Bill did so well, just reply, "He's smart, that's all," implying that this is the quality your victim lacks. If your victim says that doing well in the market is not purely a function of brains, agree with him: "You're right. It takes guts as well," naming another trait that your victim presumably lacks.

Add, in a tone of appropriate gratitude, "Bill's given me some great tips." When your victim asks if you would mind passing them along in the future, demur, "Sorry, I'm sworn to secrecy." When the stock market takes a tumble, your victim may eagerly ask if Bill is taking a shellacking. Reply, "Oh, no, he's been short recently."

Every now and then, one reads about a stock that craters. Tell your victim afterwards, "Turns out Bill was short Novastar." Shake your head in amazement at his perspicacity.

If your victim makes fifty thousand a year, tell him the following story. "Bill says that just six years ago, he just was like everyone else; he had a cheesy, little job that barely paid him a hundred thousand a year, and he was going nowhere. So he decided to go out on his own and make some real money trading stocks. It took guts, but Bill says that's what it takes to really make it financially."

If your victim is an egghead who prides himself on his high IQ, add, "You know, the funny thing is, Bill only got 470 and 490 on his SATs." The thought of such a dummy running circles around him will gall your victim even more.

One crucial point to make is that Bill is younger than your victim. This always makes it worse, as if time has passed your victim by. No one ever feels envy hearing about a rich, old codger, but a rich, young one stimulates the jealousy gland directly. If your victim is a woman, just turn Bill into Wilhemina. Same-sex accomplishment also has a more direct effect upon the gland.

Add, "Bill says it's not about the money. He just trades stocks because he enjoys it." The thought that all that wealth is just a byproduct of a fun hobby will rankle further.

Talk about Bill's life of luxury, about how he flew a girlfriend to Las Vegas in his private jet for the weekend. Say, "They treat him like a king there. Hell, he *is* a king." Shake your head in wonderment and say, "He does like to gamble. By the way—in case you ever begin to suspect that there might be some justice in this world—he ended up winning [here, take your victim's annual salary and triple it] a hundred and fifty thousand bucks in just two days of playing craps."

Add, "Bill says he doesn't like the way people kiss his ass these days just because he has money." (This is akin to beautiful women complaining about how people can't see past their looks; it is not a plaint that evokes sympathy.) "He says that once women find out how much money he has, they'll do anything to please him." Add, with an appreciative chuckle at Bill's wild streak, "He averages about two new women a week these days."

Say, "Bill says money doesn't buy happiness though." Shrug as if you can't understand why he would insist on something so obviously untrue, and add, "He sure seems happy to me."

If your victim ever asks what Bill has been up to recently, just reply, "Living happily ever after."

The Professional

In Europe, it's "who you are" that matters, with that concept pretty much being defined as the sum of your ancestry; in America, it's what you do that defines you. Thus, your victim's occupation presents a golden opportunity to attack him where he lives. Under the guise of innocent confusion, you can always make your victim's job sound second rate.

The medical profession, for example, is rife with such opportunities.

If your victim is a psychologist, ask, "Psychiatrists are the ones who are real doctors, right?"

Likewise, if he's an optometrist, ask, "Do optometrists have to go to medical school?" When he answers no, say, "Oh, that's right, those are ophthalmologists."

If he's a dentist, ask, "I'm not saying this about you, but most dentists are just guys who couldn't get into med school, right?"

If your victim is a nurse, ask, "Did you ever think about becoming a doctor?" Gird for a long-winded explanation.

If your victim actually is a doctor, ask what kind. If he's a general practitioner, say, "My cousin is an orthopedic surgeon." If this doesn't make your victim insecure enough, add, "He's at the top of his profession," implying, of course, that your victim is not.

If your victim is an orthopedic surgeon, talk about your cousin the brain surgeon. If your victim is a brain surgeon, ask which hospital he works at. Then say, "My cousin operates out of Massachusetts General. They send him cases from all over the world," implying that he gets the cases that are too difficult for *ordinary* brain surgeons like your victim.

Unless your victim is the top brain surgeon at the top hospital in the United States, you can make him feel second rate. (Of course, the further you have to go to top him, the riskier your ploy is; in the rarefied world of brain surgeons, for instance, most have heard of each other.)

If your victim is a teacher, emphasize the low pay. Sympathize, "You know, I just don't think it's right that teachers, who are responsible for the future of our country, are valued less by our society than stockbrokers." Shake your head. "I had a cousin who was a teacher. He said he could barely make ends meet. He had to drive a secondhand car, live in a rental apartment. He absolutely hated it. He's a hedge fund manager now."

Or, just be admiring: "I think it's so noble when people like you care so little about money that you're willing to devote yourself to a profession that's so low-paid."

If your victim works in advertising, say, "I heard from my cousin who was an adman that virtually everyone in advertising wants to be doing something else. The copywriters want to be real writers, the art directors want to be real artists, the producers would rather be working on TV shows, and the account executives would rather be entrepreneurs. It's just that they aren't quite good enough to make the switch. It's not that way at your firm, is it?"

There's always a way of making your victim feel second-rate. Chances are you live in a glass house yourself, but if you pose your question innocently enough, you can throw as many rocks as you like.

After all, you're only quoting your cousin.

The Wealth Flaunter

You'll never be able to instill shame into people who show off their money, but you can at least point out why they should feel shame.

Start by saying, "I've never known anyone so desperate to show that he has money."

"You should paint an arrow on your shirt sleeve pointing down at your wrist, so nobody misses the Rolex."

"Next time you buy an expensive piece of jewelry, you really should just leave the price tag on it; just wear it around that way."

"You should have your name stenciled on the side of your Mercedes, so that even when you're not in it, people will still know it's yours."

"You should carry around a money clip with a roll of thousands and start thumbing through it every time you meet someone new."

"Have you ever heard the expression, 'The more expensive the accoutrements, the cheaper the person'?"

"You really should just carry around your brokerage statement and show everyone that. Why mess around with these halfway measures?"

"Maybe you should have your net worth silk-screened onto a T-shirt, or would even you consider that bad taste?"

"Here's what you should really do. Get a room, line all the walls with mirrors, and put a bar stool in the middle of it. Take all your money, convert it into coins, and pile it in the room. Then take off all your clothes, sit on the stool, and spin around. I have the feeling that would be nirvana for you."

The Proud Parent

Some people think it's acceptable to boast about their children because it's not really boasting about themselves. But as we all know, our children are really just extensions of ourselves. So if your victim boasts about his children, insult him—by insulting them. Since in normal social situations one is expected to gush over the child, your task is easy: any deviation from this norm will be immediately apparent.

If your victim tells you that Johnny is talking up a storm, reply, "Hmm, takes after you." (The motor mouth implication will be quite clear.)

If your victim proudly reports that Johnny is reading ahead of his grade level, ask, "How soon is he going to *write* a book?"

If your victim exults about Johnny getting straight A's, reply cryptically, "Lake Woebegone—where all the children are above average!" If he asks what you mean by that comment, just say, "Just thinking of the book, that's all. Good book—have you read it?"

If your victim reports that Johnny hit a home run in his Little League game, reply, as if you don't mean it, "You've got another Babe Ruth on your hands there." (Don't sound sarcastic, merely exhibit a total lack of enthusiasm.)

If your victim replies that Johnny's IQ was tested at 139, mildly reply, "That's good. My nephew scored 155."

If your victim reports that Johnny ran a mile in seven minutes at age nine, reply, "That's good. Hey, did you know that Kim Gallagher, a 1984 Olympian, ran a five thirty-seven when she was only eight?"

No matter what the child's accomplishment, one-up it.

Always say that the child looks like the other parent, especially if your victim is the father.

If the child is good at anything that requires practice, assume your victim is the worst kind of stage parent: "Personally, I'm going to let my child choose his own interests. I think it's really unhealthy when parents get their vicarious thrills through their children. I'm not going to deprive my kid of a normal childhood, that's for sure."

Show your concern for his child's health. If Johnny scratches his head, ask, "Have you had him checked for lice? I can't tell you how many friends have had children who've gotten those at school."

If Johnny scratches his behind, ask, "Have you had him checked for tapeworm? Those things can really be insidious."

If the child is thin and tall, suggest, "He might have Marfan syndrome. You might want to have him checked for that."

If the child is at all overweight, say, "You know, you're really doing your child a disservice by feeding him sugar when he's young. Those bad dietary habits will hurt him for the rest of his life."

If his offspring demands any attention at all, casually comment, "Spare the rod and spoil the child."

If the child exhibits a fascination with matches or has a problem with bedwetting, point out that those are two of the three things that distinguish serial killers at an early age. Say, "Of course, that doesn't *necessarily* mean that he'll turn out to be a serial killer. He's not mean to animals, is he?"

The Self-Proclaimed Brain

A certain type of person takes an inordinate pride in his IQ. No matter how little he has achieved in life, he always takes comfort in knowing he's supposed to be smart.

Everyone wants to put down the self-anointed brainiac. This is why "If you're so smart, why aren't you rich?" is such a cliché. (The reason so few people ever answer, "I *am* rich," is because rich people generally prefer to boast about their money in the first place.) In fact, as a rule, the less success your victim has had, the more he feels obliged to mention his brains. It's up to you to point out this dichotomy.

There are several ways to deflate Mr. Smartypants. If he mentions his SATs or Phi Beta Kappa membership, ask him, "Where do you think the phrase, 'It's academic,' comes from? It comes from the fact that schooling doesn't make any difference."

"There's nothing more pathetic than a guy who's thirty-one boasting about his SATs. By that age, you're supposed to have actually done something."

Drive the point home with specific examples: "Did you know that Mozart wrote his first symphony when he was a teenager? That Ken Kesey wrote *One Flew Over the Cuckoo's Nest* when he was twenty-eight? That almost every great mathematician came up with his breakthrough idea before he was thirty?"

Or respond to his boasting by saying, "Well, you are *book* smart." (Nobody ever thinks of himself as *not* street smart.)

Ask, "Have you ever heard the expression, 'The smaller the brain, the bigger the ego'?"

If your victim ever uses the word "intellectual," interrupt him with, "What is the definition of an intellectual? Someone who *thinks* he's smart."

The most pathetic brainiacs are those who take the trouble to join MENSA. If your victim tells you he belongs, reply, "Oh yeah, I've seen you guys at the airports, with your tambourines and stuff."

After he tells you that you're thinking of the Hare Krishnas, and that MENSA is an organization for the high-IQed, reply, "Oh yeah, that's right, I hear you have to be in the upper 2 percent of the population to join." After he puffs up with pride at this recognition, ask, "What's the organization for the top 1 percent called?" Then tell him the answer: "It's called the multi-millionaires' club."

The Aging Athlete

The aging athlete's overwhelming purpose in life is to prove that he is every bit as good as he was when he was young. Your overwhelming purpose is to remind him of how old he really is.

If your victim is between the ages of thirty and fifty, and he's in great physical shape even by the standards of twenty-year-olds, tell him, "You're in good shape for your age." Those last three words will drain all the pleasure out of the compliment.

Many men, upon being given such "compliments," feel obliged to point out that they're not what they once were (to let you know that once upon a time, they were *really* something). Agree: "Well, the old lion *is* getting a little long in the tooth." If he recoils, rapidly backtrack: "No, I just mean, you look very ... distinguished." (This last word, with its implications of age, is of course a dirty word in his lexicon.)

Tell him, "You know, at your age, you really shouldn't be exercising so hard. You could have a heart attack or a stroke."

After he protests that he's as fit as ever, remonstrate: "Come on, you can't expect to keep up with the young bucks anymore."

At some point, he may feel obliged to get back on the court and demonstrate his prowess. At first, say, "Wow, the old man still has it." Then wrinkle your brow and ask, "You're not bothered at all by arthritis, are you?" After he says no, and asks why you ask, respond, "It's just ... never mind, it's nothing."

If he does hurt himself, say, "I have to say, as a friend, it pains me to see you spending your declining years trying to recapture the lost glory of your youth."

After he protests, add, "In ten years you'll be ___." (Whatever age that will sound very old to him.) Say, "At that point, you at least want to be alive and kicking. At the rate you're going ..."

Later on, if you catch him examining himself in the locker room mirror, look at his midsection and say, consolingly, "Listen, everybody, no matter how hard they exercise, gets middle-age spread. It's inevitable." If you can get away with it, gently pull out some of his skin and say, "I know the name of a good doctor who specializes in tummy tucks." (Don't say "liposuction"; "tummy tucks" sound more feminine.) Add, "I think he does mostly women though."

Men like this often try to feel youthful by talking about, or even trying to pick up, younger women. Gently chide, "Come on, they must look at you as a father figure."

Add, "By the way, I hope you're getting your prostate checked every year."

The Tiresome Comedian

Your victim may fancy himself a wit because he tells jokes (the kind that get recited, not witty situational asides). The classic putdowns have always been, "Don't give up your day job" and "You ought to fire your writers," but these are overused. There are better ways to make your victim feel foolish.

Just listen to his joke stone-faced, then, a few seconds after he delivers the punch line, give a barely perceptible nod.

Or interrupt your victim to deliver the punch line yourself, but say it in such an extremely bored tone that it is clear you don't find the joke funny. Your victim starts out, "A proctologist was walking down a hospital corridor when someone stopped him and asked, 'Hey doc, what are you doing with that rectal thermometer behind your ear?'" You yawn, "Yeah, yeah, I know, he pulls it out and says some asshole's got my pencil."

Another solution is to start laughing wildly at the setup, then not laugh at the punch line, and give him a "What happened then?" look.

Another response is simply to interrupt him mid-joke and say, "Oh shoot, I gotta phone my stockbroker." Whip out your cell phone and place a fake call. Then, after he has waited patiently for a minute or two for you to hang up, just start talking about the stock market. If he tries to finish his joke, interrupt again the same way.

As he tells his joke, make an impatient circular motion with your hand, as if trying to get him to hurry up. At the end, just ask, "You done?"

After your victim tells you a long-winded, supposedly humorous anecdote, don't crack a smile. Instead, remind him, "Brevity is the soul of wit."

If your victim makes the kind of lame joke that effete people like to titter at to prove they get the joke, respond thusly: "For humor to really be funny, it somehow has to relate to our deepest desires, shames, and fears. The funniest jokes are often the ugliest, the ones that go directly against what society condones. Sorry, but your weak little jokes just don't do it for me."

If his joke actually is funny, and you don't mind appearing a twit, act put out by his political incorrectness. Primly say, "There are a lot of people who would find that really offensive."

If he makes an ethnic joke, tell him you're part whatever group he just made a joke about, and bristle.

Perhaps the best solution is forced laughter, not so much as to appear you are making fun of him, but enough that it is evident you are trying to be polite. Keep the smile fixed a few moments too long (real smiles are fleeting; false ones linger longer). This will really make him feel foolish.

The Tough Guy

After the wannabe tough guy has tried to demonstrate his toughness (you can count on him to do this on a regular basis), merely say:

"Do you eat railroad spikes for breakfast?"

"You should enter that World's Strongest Man competition they have on ESPN."

"Man, you must have testicles the size of grapefruits!"

If he hunts, ask, "You use a gun? I figured you for the type who would chase a deer down in the woods, catch it with his bare hands, then strangle it and eat its raw meat right there on the spot."

But the best way to mock him is to psychoanalyze him. Ask, "Why is it so important for you to be tough? All of the truly tough guys I've ever known haven't really cared about whether they were tough or not. The guys who want to appear tough are always those who came from the more sheltered backgrounds."

Ask, "What exactly is it you're trying to compensate for? It comes across as if you have a strong inferiority complex that drives you to do these things."

Continue, "Psychologists say that a lot of these 'tough guys' are just latent homosexuals who are trying to convince themselves that they're real men. In fact, they say that most gay men go through a stage in their lives where they try desperately to be macho before they finally resign themselves to their homosexuality."

Finish up with this bit of helpful advice: "You should learn to relax and act like a normal, sane person."

The Braggart

After your victim has bragged about something, anything, the best response is simply to say, "Okay—if you say so." This doesn't quite rise to the level of a challenge, but does express quite clearly that you don't believe him, or at the very least don't take him seriously.

Let's say your victim asserts that he's the best negotiator at his law firm. A similarly mild response is, "Well, that's one way of looking at it."

Or just look taken aback, pause for a second as if searching for something positive to say, then just say, "Okay." The tepidness of your response will be very eloquent.

Or laugh, then pause, look at him again, and say, "Oh, sorry, you're being serious."

Or, "You're cute," as if he is but a child indulging in fantasy.

The usual response in this situation is to say, "Dream on." But that is unmistakably antagonistic. Instead, try, "That's a harmless enough daydream, I suppose."

Or, "I guess you're not hurting anyone with that illusion."

Or, in a very reasonable tone, "Far be it from me to burst your delusions."

Your best opportunity comes if someone else is present, and your victim has been boasting to both of you. Before the third person has a chance to respond, quickly cut him off by saying, "Don't laugh! We're all entitled to our little pretensions." This is particularly effective because it makes clear that you assume that the third person's reaction was going to be derision, effectively making him your collaborator. And by saying this quickly and harshly—and you must sound very serious—at first it seems as if you're sticking up for your victim, when in fact you're doing the exact opposite.

The Person Who
Thinks He's Special

There's no better way to burst Mr. Unique's bubble than to say, "I've met a lot of guys like you before."

After he acts in some quintessentially conceited way, thinking he's just proven that he's better than everyone else, just shake your head slightly, and say wearily, "Back where I come from, there are a lot of guys like you." Your message will be very clear: not only is he nothing special, you find him quite tiresome to boot. He can't possibly interpret this comment in a positive light, since no one thinks that someone who's good in any way is a common type.

Add, "There were a million guys like you at my high school. It's as if you all took the same course in how to act in public." This statement not only makes him common, it also demotes him back to high school.

There are limitless variations on this theme:

"I can't even count the number of guys I've met who are just like you." Smile wryly and say, "They all thought they were something pretty special." You needn't add, "But they weren't." It would be redundant.

Or, "... and they all wore their egos on their sleeve." If your victim thinks he's something special, he undoubtedly does the same.

Or, "I knew a guy like you once ... Everybody hated him." On the surface, this is not quite a personal attack since you yourself aren't expressing an opinion, other than the assumption that "everybody" probably includes you. But it is all the more devastating since it implies that "everybody" would hate your victim given the opportunity, making opinion against him unanimous.

Or just laugh at him, showing you don't take him seriously, and offer, "Guys like you are a dime a dozen."

Forget His Name

There's no clearer way to let your egotistical victim know that he barely registers on your radar screen than to not remember his name no matter how many times you see him.

When it's time to introduce him to someone else, act flustered, and say, "I'm sorry, I know your name perfectly well, it's just for some reason I seem to be drawing a blank on it right now ..." Your embarrassment shows you're not just doing this for effect. Manfully take the blame by saying, "I must be having a senior moment."

Next time you see your victim, instead of greeting him by name, say "Hey buddy!" This makes it quite plain that you can't remember his name.

Other greetings:

"Hey tiger!"

"Hey slick!"

"Hey man!"

"Hey big guy!"

Or just, "Hey!"

Or call him the name of some famous person of his ethnicity. For example, if he's Italian, call him Frank Sinatra, or Mussolini, or Luciano Pavarotti, or Topo Gigio. Even worse, just call him by any given Italian name: Salvatore, or Vincenzo, or Giuseppe.

After a while, he'll get the message that you don't consider him worth remembering.

Get Him Confused with Someone Else

Never ask your victim specific questions that indicate you remember anything about him. If the last time you saw him he was about to perform at Carnegie Hall, don't ask how it went. Talk instead about how long the line was at Stop & Shop that morning.

If he does bring up his performance, give a vague, "Oh yeah ... What instrument do you play again?" Then, as he tells you, look off in the distance as if thinking about something else. At the end of his spiel, respond, "So, what have you been up to recently?"

If you must ask your victim about himself, ask him if he's been riding much recently. He'll respond, "What?" Clarify, "You know, on your horse." When he replies that he doesn't ride horses, say, "I must have you confused with somebody else."

Add, by way of apology, "I'm sorry, you're the type I get confused with other people."

If he tells you about an argument he had with his wife, respond, "Oh yeah, you're married, aren't you ..."

When he tells you what his children have been doing, ask, "You have kids?"

Lest he ascribe your inability to remember anything about him to a congenitally weak memory, demonstrate with a third party—in front of your victim—that you have perfect recall. Ask this third party about his kids (all of whose names you remember), ask about their various hobbies, and even mention that one of them has a birthday coming up soon.

You really can't rob your victim of anything more basic than his identity.

Make it Clear You're Not Listening to Him

When your egomaniacal victim starts to talk about himself, just tune out. This is most easily accomplished when you're traveling in a car together. Whenever he tries to talk, reach over and absentmindedly turn up the volume on the radio. You can even ask him questions before you do this, demonstrating how interested you are in his answers.

If you're not in a car, and the two of you are standing, just start to do exercises while he's talking. Move your head from side to side, as if working out a kink in your neck, or do arm stretches, or bend down and touch your toes. Any sort of calisthenic will make it clear that you're more focused on your own body than you are on him.

Or just start fiddling with whatever is at hand. Pick up a leaflet and idly glance through it while your victim is speaking.

Open your wallet and silently count the bills.

Look at a distant billboard.

Frequently consult your watch.

If your victim ever asks in exasperation, "Are you listening to me?" reply, "Yeah … yeah. You're telling me about how your car wouldn't start the other morning, right?" Then look away and do some deep knee bends.

If you want to demonstrate your strong family values, pull out your wallet and gaze fondly at the pictures of your children while he's talking to you.

Withhold Eye Contact

Eye contact is one of the most intimate of human experiences. Lovers from time immemorial have gazed rapturously into each other's eyes. Poets claim that the eye is the window to the soul. And staring is usually a dead giveaway that you admire someone's looks.

The reverse is also true: when you don't look directly at somebody, it's often because you don't like him. The best thing about withholding eye contact is that it communicates this message unmistakably, yet so subtly your egocentric victim will be unaware of how you are doing it, and will thus be doubly disconcerted.

Give your victim exactly the same amount of eye contact he would get from you on the phone. Look past him as if he doesn't exist. Look at everyone else in the room, but not him, as if every other person in the room is more interesting (or at least visually appealing) than he is. Face your victim, so that the lack of eye contact will be more obvious. (If you're side by side, the message may be lost.) If a third party comes up to speak to you, look him directly in the eye and smile.

This technique is at its most lethal when there are four of you sitting at a dinner table. During the course of the meal, look back and forth between the other two, never letting your eyes rest upon your victim. You'll be surprised by how disconcerted he will become.

At some point, your victim may blurt out, "Is something wrong? You seem very distant." Look right past him and distractedly reply, "No."

A related technique is to lightly hold the tip of your nose with your thumb and forefinger each time your victim speaks, as if his words give off a bad odor. (The idea is not to hold your nose as you would if trying to send the message directly; just lightly touch it as if unaware of your own body language.)

A variation on this technique is to seemingly unconsciously put your finger to your lips whenever your victim speaks, as if telling him, "Shush."

Or just wince ever so slightly whenever he opens his mouth.

When these techniques have the desired effect, your victim will be filled with a vague unease. Don't be surprised if he feels a desperate need to assert himself somehow. (If he does, it will probably be with some blundering move, which is easily parried or put down.)

PART II

Appearances

"I Saw Someone Who Looks Exactly Like You!"

Most men, in some secret compartment of their mind, imagine they bear a slight resemblance to Sean Connery (or Brad Pitt or Mario Van Peebles). Any actual resemblance to Peter Lorre (or Elton John or Al Sharpton) never seems to register. Similarly, women will often see a trace of Wynona Ryder in their features, never recognizing their closer resemblance to Roseanne. (These misimpressions are always exacerbated because people always look at their best angle in the mirror—which is why we all tend to think that photographs of us are bad.) So whenever we're told that someone looks exactly like us, when we actually see the other person, we usually find the comparison less than flattering.

Pick someone who looks slightly like your victim, but is slightly shorter, fatter, frizzier, and more pig-faced. Then, in front of both of them, point out the resemblance. Your target will seethe, his anger exacerbated by the fact that he can only suffer in silence. Unless he's incredibly rude, he can't very well blurt out, "I don't look like him! I'm much handsomer!" (He can't even say that later on without sounding foolish.)

You can only hope that your victim's "look-alike," pleased by the comparison, agrees wholeheartedly.

Add, "Ah well, they say we all have a doppelganger somewhere. I guess it's true."

Later on, your victim may ask, "I don't really look like him, do I?" Reply, "Well, I guess he *is* a little more muscular."

Your victim may then plaintively ask, "But I'm better-looking than him, aren't I?" Reply, "Yeah, I guess he's only a four; you're at least a five." (However your victim would rank on a scale of ten, take him down a couple notches.)

He may say, "I'm only a five?" Reply, "I said *at least* a five."

At some point, your victim will ask, "Come on, you're joking, right?" Reply, "What's the problem? He's not that bad looking."

Saying this is effectively reaching into his chest cavity and pushing his heart down a few inches.

Fatso

Hounding someone for physical flaws is, of course, completely unjustified. But sometimes nasty people also have physical flaws, in which case you can feel justified using those flaws to wound them.

At first, call attention to your victim's weight problem by seeming to refer to it inadvertently. If you want to indicate low odds for an outcome, say, "Fat chance." If your victim comes by a windfall, say, "Wow! You're living in Fat City!" Show that you need a challenge by saying, "I don't want to just get fat and happy." Tell him you want to drop out of the rat race and move to the country and "live off the fat of the land." Each time you use the word, glance momentarily at his midsection.

If a lean person happens by, compliment him effusively for being "lean and mean," for "caring about himself," and for having "the discipline not to let himself turn into an eyesore." Even after he's gone, enthuse about how good he looks.

Eat candy in front of your victim. Munch away with a look of transport, then complain, "You know, no matter how hard I try, I can't seem to gain any weight."

If your victim mentions his diet, refer to studies that show that over 95 percent of people who diet gain all their weight back within two years.

If your victim complains about his weight problem without mentioning a number, guess his weight. If he looks around two-fifty, say, "Hey, it's not like you weigh two-fifty or anything." If he then admits to weighing that much, just say, "Oh well, it's not as if you weight two-seventy."

Or say, "Billy and I were arguing the other day. How much do you weigh?" Finding out that other people have been discussing his weight behind his back is sure to depress him.

When you pass a scale, insist he get on, as if you don't believe that he weighs what he claims.

Suggest liposuction to him. Then add, "But a lot of people complain that they end up looking lumpy afterwards, that the fat wasn't taken out evenly."

Ask if airlines make him buy two tickets.

Refer to him as Minnesota, Mr. Domino, and Mr. Waller. (He may not get it at first, but eventually he'll realize that you are referring to Minnesota Fats, Fats Domino, and Fats Waller.)

Ask your victim if he can see his genitals when he looks down, or if he needs a mirror to see them.

If your victim is female, talk about another female—who has a smaller derriere—and say she "would be attractive except that she's a little big in the caboose." Belabor the point by referring to it as a "huge turd cutter," "enormous fart box," and "gigantic mud flaps."

If you feel bad about this, just tell yourself you're practicing "tough love." ("Tough love" is the excuse of choice for closet sadists everywhere.)

The overwhelming preponderance of recent evidence indicates that fatness is genetic, that it's primarily a function of how many fat cells one is born with, and that the only way for a fat person to lose weight is by starving his fat cells. In other words, it's pretty much beyond his control. Nonetheless, do your best to make him feel guilty.

If you ever do shame your victim into losing weight, be sure to take all the credit.

Skinny

A few skinny people are anorexic or bulimic, but the rest simply have no choice. So act as if you assume your skinny victim is anorexic or bulimic.

If your victim is male, comment, "I thought only girls got anorexia." When he denies being anorexic, just ignore him and ask, "So how long have you been anorexic?"

Ask, "What's that called when you make yourself throw up after every meal—oh, that's right, bulimia. Don't you find all that bile wears the enamel off your teeth?"

"When you look in the mirror, do you see a fat person?" Add, "Because you're not, you know. In fact, you're really thin."

Or you can compliment him for being thin, as if it was his goal in life to be a beanpole: "You are really lean and mean." Then give him the once over and add, "I mean, *really* lean."

The word "skinny" is not nearly as bad as "scrawny," but you can turn it into a bad word by apologizing for it: "You are so skinny—sorry, I mean thin. I mean, sorry, you know, slender." Tiptoe around the concept as if it is some extremely shameful condition you must euphemize.

After your victim explains that his is a genetic condition he has little control over, helpfully suggest, "You should eat more, gain some weight," as if this had never occurred to him before.

If he says he eats three square meals a day, ask, "What do you have for dinner, a pea?" Add, "You should weight lift … or something."

Compliment a more muscular guy by saying, "Bill is built like a brick shithouse! He's a real man—you know, a full size guy."

Say, "They say you can never be too rich or too thin." Then, after glancing at him, amend your statement: "Well, never too rich, anyway."

Look at your victim and say, "You know, in Africa, they call AIDS 'the skinny disease.'"

After your victim denies having AIDS, say, "Oh, I wasn't saying you had full-blown AIDS ... But you know, even when you're just HIV-positive, you can start to lose weight."

After your victim denies being HIV-positive, say, "Okay, don't be so sensitive; I wasn't implying you were." Then, with a look of concern, ask, "So how's your T-cell count?"

After he vehemently denies that he is HIV-positive, say, "Okay, okay." But when he gets near, shy away as if afraid of touching him.

One thing you don't have to worry about with your skinny victim is getting beaten up afterwards.

Short

If tall people feel they are sore thumbs, short people tend to view their height as an open, gaping wound. Pour some salt in your victim's.

Use the word "stature" to describe people's standing in life. Say that others "look up" to a widely admired person. When describing a failure, say that someone "didn't measure up."

After a faux pas, say, "Ouch. I feel like I'm about five inches tall." Then give him a quick look and wince, as if you realize you've just compounded your error.

When speaking to your victim, stand as close to him as possible, so he has to look up to you.

If your victim is five feet six inches, and you're six feet, wistfully say, "Man, I'd love to be six and a half feet tall. That'd be such an advantage in life, to have everybody notice you and look up to you like that."

Be lamely complimentary about his height. Say, "You probably would have made a really good gymnast." Or, "You could probably do really well as a jockey."

Or say, "You're so lucky, you can get clothes more cheaply." When he looks at you questioningly, explain, "You can fit into boys' sizes."

At some point, your victim may admit that he hates being short. Be sympathetic and agreeable: "Yeah, you're right, I bet being short really sucks. I'd hate to go through my entire life being short." Add, "Hey, I thought you people didn't like being called short anymore. I thought you preferred 'vertically challenged.'"

Ask, "How tall are your parents? Did you not drink any milk as a child? Did you start smoking early or something?"

Ask, "How tall are you?" When he tells you, look doubtful.

Helpfully point out, "You know, girls would like you if you weren't so short. You actually have an okay-looking face."

If a group of you are in a crowd, offer to lift him up so he can see. When you get to a restaurant, put a telephone book on his seat. If he's giving a speech, rather than adjust the mike downward for him, put a stool on the platform so he can stand on it.

When he boasts, reply, "Wow—that must make you feel six feet tall."

When he finally snaps at you, comment, "You have the worst Napoleonic complex I've ever seen."

If there are other people around, say, "Hey, Victim, stand up. Oh, sorry, you're already standing up."

Then apologize: "I'm sorry, I always get them confused—are you a midget or a dwarf?"

Tall

Being tall is generally considered an advantage, but tall people are often surprisingly self-conscious about their height; you can make your tall victim even more so.

Ask your victim if he's acromegalic. He will probably say he's not, and will explain to you that acromegaly is a special medical condition resulting in the forehead, nose, and jaw continuing to grow even after the person has stopped growing, resulting in a face like Andre the Giant's. Reply, "I know—that's why I was asking."

Say enviously, "Man, you have the greatest pickup line in the world." When he asks what that is, reply, "I'm proportionate." He will then probably have to explain that this is not so. If he doesn't, ask, "It *is* true, isn't it?" forcing him to reply.

When he was in junior high school and high school, your victim was undoubtedly tormented by other students who called him, "Lurch," "Frankenstein," "Chewbacca," and so on. Show him that those days are not entirely gone.

If your victim is a woman, it's even easier to torment her. All you have to do is spell out the awkwardness inherent in her life. Ask, "When you date men of average height, do they have to stand on their tiptoes to kiss you?"

Tell her, "You have a great build for swimming," (or basketball). These are hardly the feminine ideal, and chances are she will not be flattered.

Conclude, "You should have been a guy; you would have made a great guy."

If that doesn't seem to sting, add, "I think you were meant to be a guy, things just got a little confused in the womb."

Ugly

It bears repeating that someone's appearance is absolutely no reason to pick on him. But if your victim is ugly as well as mean, use his looks to get back at him.

If you want to hurt your victim, don't hurl a blatant insult at him ("you ugly bastard"). Instead, offer false sympathy: "Some people are so superficial—all they care about is looks."

Say, "I'm not the kind of person who just looks at a person's face and judges him on that." Then put a self-satisfied look on, as if you expect him to get down on his knees and thank you for seeing past his ugly mug.

Add, "After I've known someone awhile, I don't even notice their looks anymore," as if this will make him feel better about himself.

If your victim is fully grown, offer the following: "Maybe you're like that duckling. Maybe you'll grow into a beautiful swan."

If you pass by a mirror, look at your victim, then blurt out, as if you expect to establish a common bond this way, "I hate mirrors! I just hate them! You know what I mean?" Adding the "You know what I mean" puts him in an awkward spot because he must either agree with you, tacitly acknowledging his own ugliness, or disagree, implying that he likes his looks.

If you really want to depress your victim, glumly give the following speech, as if you are disheartened by it yourself: "Looks are everything in life, you know what I mean? Much as we'd like to think differently, they determine our status starting in elementary school, and it never stops. Good-looking people get the best sex partners, the best jobs, the best everything. It sucks, it really sucks. Even with presidential elections, they've done studies that show it's usually the better-looking guy who wins." Shake your head at the hopelessness of the situation. Then add, "And those people who say they're not influenced by looks—they're the ones who are the most influenced of all."

Handsome

The best way to insult someone who's good-looking, or at least thinks he is, is to let him know that you think he isn't. Don't say this overtly ("I don't know why other people think you're so good-looking, I don't think you are"), he'll probably interpret that (correctly) as indirect flattery. Instead, just say something that implies he's not that good-looking, which is a much more powerful statement because no insult is intended.

Say to your victim, "[A mutual acquaintance] is *so* good-looking. I'd love to go through just one day of my life looking like that guy, just to see what it was like. Wouldn't you?" This puts your victim in a very awkward position. He can't say, "No, I already know what it's like," because that would make him sound like a conceited fop. So he must at least nod in agreement, which is tacit acknowledgment that he is not as good-looking.

Add, "His friends tell me he's never once been turned down by a girl." This is tangible proof that the other fellow is better looking, because your victim has undoubtedly been turned down. (The only reason a guy, no matter how good-looking, would never have been turned down by a girl is because he's gay.)

If your victim is dark, explain your mutual acquaintance's powers of attraction by saying, "He has blond hair and blue eyes, you know what I mean?" If your victim is blond and of medium height, point out, "You know how it is with guys who are tall, dark, and handsome."

Add, "The funny thing is, there are so many people who think they're good-looking when they're not. That's one of the things I like about you, you're not that way."

Then conclude, "Ah, I guess looks are a mixed blessing anyway. I have this theory that good-looking people never develop personalities. All their lives, people treat them well because they're good-looking, so they sort of develop these passive personalities and never amount to much. Know what I mean?"

If at any point your victim ever protests that he thinks he's actually pretty good-looking, laugh, clap him on the shoulder, and say, "You're all right," as if he's just made a good joke. If you can't laugh on command, instead shoot him a disbelieving look, then forever after call him "Narcissus."

Beautiful

The key to getting to a beautiful woman is that she probably doesn't think she's all that good-looking. (The average man tends to think himself much better looking than he actually is, while the average woman tends to think herself worse looking. One of the side effects of testosterone seems to be overconfidence; estrogen, on the other hand, seems to confer insecurity.)

Start by saying, "A lot of people seem to think you're quite good-looking." Say it in a tone of voice that indicates you're not of that opinion. She will probably respond by pointing out some flaw(s) of hers, real or imagined. Don't agree with her—that would be rude. Instead, simply spend the rest of your time with her staring at it. When she sees you doing so, look away quickly, as you would if caught staring at the stump of an amputee. Then watch her slowly crumble in front of your eyes.

Another approach, if your victim is in her thirties, is to mention how you've heard that it's much harder for beautiful women to age, since they have much more to lose. Be sympathetic: "It's just so unfair that women are judged by their looks so much more than men. They say that in Hollywood, an actress's career is over by forty, unless they want to play character roles. A lot of them seem to get plastic surgery. But it never really works; they never really look that good again."

The other tack to take is to say, "I've actually talked to a number of psychiatrists who say that being beautiful really stunts a woman. They never really figure out who they are, since people see only the surface and never really pay attention to the real them."

If You Know She's
Had Plastic Surgery

How you approach the recent plastic surgery patient depends on whether she's admitted to her procedure. If she has admitted to her surgery, you must confine yourself to comments such as:

"Now that you've had your nose done, maybe you should think about your chin too."

"How soon before you need another facelift?"

"You think it was worth it?" (Look doubtful.)

"I think I liked you better before."

You can have even more fun with the person who doesn't want to admit it. Cosmetic surgery has much less of a stigma attached than it did twenty years ago, but a lot of people still don't like to own up to it.

Say, "You look great," then peer closely at her as if you realize something is different, but you're not sure what it is. Knit your brows and stare at her in consternation; this will cause her discomfort. When she tries to change the subject, don't let her.

If she's had a facelift, say, "You look really well rested. Have you been getting a lot of sleep recently?" When she says yes, say, "Well, make sure you keep getting your rest. It seems to have taken years off your face."

If she's had liposuction, exclaim, "Look at you! You're one of the few people who've actually had the discipline to stick with their diets. Congratulations—you must have a lot of willpower." If she doesn't answer, ask, "Do you?" This will force her to attribute her weight loss to her superior force of will.

If she's had a facial feature altered, just stare at her closely and say, "I don't know why, but you just haven't seemed like yourself recently."

If she's had a breast augmentation, say, "There's something about you that's different, I just can't quite put my finger on it," while making a tapping motion with your finger at about the level of her breasts.

Conclude, "I would guess that you'd had plastic surgery, but you're not like that, you have good values. Someone has to be incredibly vain to go to the hospital and have a major operation just to look better. Know what I mean?"

If you have one available, pull out an old photo and hold it alongside her, comparing. Then look as if you've had a revelation, but don't say anything. This will make her squirm even more.

Helpfully Suggest
Plastic Surgery

One of the best ways to point out your victim's various defects is to suggest—as a friend, of course—how he could improve on them. Now, most people will never get plastic surgery because of the expense, the pain, and the potential embarrassment. So it's not as if he'll take your "friendly" advice. But he will get to hear about his various ugly features.

Apropos of nothing, make the following general statement: "You know, I don't think there's any shame in having plastic surgery. I mean, if I had a couple of features I wasn't happy about, I'd just go ahead and do it." This ham-handed way of suggesting he take that drastic measure is sure to offend. Add, "A lot of people get a fresh start that way."

Then say, "You're basically a good-looking guy, but you'd be even better looking if ..." It will be hard for your victim to take offense, because you've started out with a compliment. But if you offer enough suggestions, the message will eventually get through that all of his features need work, which of course means he's not good-looking.

So say, "... you'd be even better looking if you got a nose job, sculpted that thing down a little."

"... if you had your ears pinned back."

"... if you had your eyes lifted."

"... if you had a chin implant."

"... if you had some Botox injections to get rid of that permanent sneer."

"... if you had some cheekbone implants."

"… if you had some collagen injections in your lips."
"… if you had some liposuction."
After enough of this, there's only one conclusion he can draw.

The Fashion Victim

The general rule is, the more of a statement your victim is making, the easier it is to deride his outfit. But even when he's not making an obvious statement, he's saying something.

If your victim is dressed in form-fitting clothes, say, "Just have to show off that body, don't you?" Add, "I'm amazed you can get that shirt on and off without ripping it … How many pairs of jeans do you have to try on before you find a pair that fits that tight?"

If his sleeves are a little short, say, "You look like a ninth grader still trying to fit into his seventh-grade clothes."

If your victim is wearing loose-fitting clothes, say, "You look like a little kid trying on his father's clothes."

If he is dressed in clashing colors, ask, "How did you ever get your driver's license if you're color-blind?"

If he's dressed in black: "Going to a funeral?"

If he's dressed loudly: "Need a lot of attention, don't you?"

If his clothes have wrinkles: "That slept-in look really becomes you."

If he's wearing a leather jacket: "Wow, a tough guy!" If he's wearing leather pants, you needn't say anything; a smirk will suffice.

If your victim is wearing a suit, say, "Wow, that fits you like the proverbial cheap suit." Feel the fabric, then add, "Oh, I guess it is."

If your victim is a woman who is wearing a low-cut dress, comment, "Really proud of those things, aren't you?" If her décolletage is obviously expensive, say, "You look like an expensive hooker." If it's less expensive, tell her, "You look like a streetwalker."

If she's over the age of thirty but dresses younger, ask, "You really think you're young enough to get away with that?"

If she likes to wear a little jewelry and a scarf, say, "You've certainly got that fortune-teller look down pat."

If your victim (of either sex) is dressed sloppily, go to town: "Trying to disguise yourself as a wino? I guess grunge is making a comeback ... Is this what's called 'hobo chic'?"

"I guess by dressing so shabbily, you're making the statement that you don't care about clothes, that you're not a superficial person, is that it? I guess you're a deep person with good values."

If he's actually dressed well, ask, "Isn't there such a thing as trying too hard?"

If a group of you are all dressed up in tuxedoes, point out what the tuxedo does for each guy. Say to the largest guy, "You look like Paul Bunyan no matter what you wear." Point to the athlete and say, "You look like an ex-football player at the Heisman Trophy Award dinner." Point to the handsome one and say, "You look like a gigolo." Point to the intelligent one and say, "You look like a diplomat at an embassy function." Then point to your victim and say, "You look like the head-waiter at an all-you-can-eat diner." When he shoots back, "Oh, and who do you suppose you look like?" just hum the James Bond theme.

PART III
Sex and Sexuality

His Girlfriend

If your victim's girlfriend is good-looking, he probably likes to show her off. After he's done so, point out, "Good-looking women are usually shallow, selfish, and spoiled. But I'm sure she's not that way." (This will underline the fact that she probably is.)

Or say in a congratulatory fashion, "Way to go, Johnny baby—I hear she's really loose!" (This is what a guy wants to hear before he beds a girl, not after.)

Or send the same message another way: "She looks like she could suck a basketball through a garden hose!"

If the girl is not particularly good-looking (this description encompasses 90 percent of us), causing your victim discomfiture is easy. Once you get him alone, get straight to the point: "You find her attractive?"

Praise your victim's character: "I'm glad to see you're not the superficial type. Looks aren't that important anyway." If he takes offense, protest, "What are you getting mad about? I'm giving you a compliment!"

Compliment your victim's masculinity: "I gotta hand it to you, you have a stronger sex drive than me!"

Or say, "Hmm. She's a very ... *handsome* woman, isn't she?" (No pretty woman is ever described this way, and "handsome" implies your victim has his mitts on a creature of indeterminate gender.)

Say, "You must be the first boyfriend she's ever had," with its implication that no other guy would have wanted her. When your victim heatedly denies that, follow up with, "Oh, so she's been around?" Your victim will then have to backtrack the other way.

Confide, "I don't blame you for going with a girl for whom there's not too much competition. It's *hard* to find a girl you can trust these days."

Or take the hearty approach. Say, "Hey—I guess they all look the same in the dark, eh?" and give your victim a playful punch.

Offer this seemingly neutral observation: "Hmm. She's a rather … big-boned woman, isn't she?" Many fat women blame their problems on "big bones," so the phrase has become synonymous with fatness. (By the way, when was the last time you saw a fat skeleton?)

Shake your head and say, *"De gustibus non est disputandem."* If he's not sophisticated, say it in English: "There's no accounting for taste." If he's proud of his sophistication, say it in Latin, then translate it into English for him.

Or insult your victim's masculinity: "Gee—she looks like she'd be a little too much woman for you." Your victim may respond with, "Are you saying I'm not enough man for her?" Answer, "No, no, just that she's a lot of woman, that's all." (This merely shifts the focus of the insult to her weight.)

Her Boyfriend

Women are less visual in their choice of mates, but they will get just as defensive if you insult their boyfriends on the same basis.

After you meet him, casually ask, "Was he your first choice?" After she insists he was, peer at her closely, as if trying to determine if she is lying. Then say, as if to make up for your rudeness, "Well, he looks … intelligent."

Add, "But I thought you liked them tall, dark, and handsome." After she says something to the effect that looks aren't that important to her, and anyway, she thinks he's cute, reply, "Ooooh, I see—he's rich."

At this point, she will either say he is, but that she would like him anyway, or that he's not and money isn't that important to her. If it's the former, say disbelievingly, "Riiiiight." If it's the latter, say, as if you're making excuses for him, "If you say so. Well, he must have a good sense of humor or something."

Look perplexed for a few moments. Then ask, in a tone of disbelief, "You really get it on with that guy?" Put your hand over your mouth and half-stifle a laugh. "I can't imagine he's any good in the sack." At this point, your victim will have to either remain silent, mutely acknowledging the truth of your comment, or defend him. If she does the latter, ask for particulars: "How so? What does he do for you? Is he good at oral sex? He seems like he'd be a little klutzy to me." If she says, "None of your business," take this as evidence that you were right ("I thought so.") If she does give you particulars, she is embarrassing herself by doing so.

Conclude, in a big-brotherly tone, "You can do better than that."

If He Has No Love Life

Nothing quite spells L-O-S-E-R like not getting laid. If your victim has been high and dry recently, underline his status with a show of false sympathy.

Start this conversation by saying to your victim, "You should be going out more than you are. You're not *that* bad-looking."

Continue, "It's nothing to be ashamed of just because you never go out." (If it didn't occur to him to be ashamed before, it will now.)

Ask, "Why do you think you have such a hard time getting dates?" This question calls for a little self-flagellation, which is always fun to observe.

Wrinkle your brow and ask, diffidently, "Are you a virgin?" After he strenuously denies this, ask, "When was the last time you got laid?"

Helpfully suggest, "Maybe you should join a church group. Or a singles group. Or advertise on the Internet." (Advertising always implies last-ditch desperation.)

Say, "I don't think it's fair that just because you don't go out on dates, people think you're gay." Then, as if something just occurred to you, hastily add, "Not that there's anything wrong with being gay."

After he denies this, say, "You might as well just join a monastery." (For a woman, just substitute "nunnery.")

If your victim is a woman, say, "You poor thing, you must be so horny ... I bet you masturbate a lot."

When she denies this, act as if you don't believe her, but sympathize thusly: "You know, I just don't understand why men don't appreciate you more. Guys are so superficial. All they want is blonde hair and big tits. You have a different kind of beauty, that's all."

If your victim takes this as a compliment, angrily condemn men this way: "It's just not fair! You're lower than garbage—at least garbage gets taken out once a week!" (This is a phrase sure to haunt her forever.)

Always conclude, "Don't give up hope. Somewhere out there is a guy who would appreciate you." The implication here is that there is one person (and only one) who would like your victim—although for all you know, he may live in the middle of the Gobi desert, live in a yurt, and smell of yak butter.

If She Has a Slight Reputation

You can always leave a woman feeling slightly disgruntled by implying that she has had a past. Even women who decry society's hypocrisy on this matter are susceptible to this line of insult.

Bring up the unfairness of the double standard yourself, but say it as if you're defending *her*: "It's just not fair that men who sleep with a lot of women are admired and called studs, whereas women who sleep with a lot of men are called whores." Nod at her, as if clumsily attempting to gain her approval.

Add, "Don't worry, I'm not the kind of guy who divides all women into either pristine, nice girls or whores," making it clear which category you put her in.

Continue, "Guys who want to marry a virgin are crazy. They're better off with a woman who's had some experience—know what I mean?"

"You must really look down on girls who've had very little sexual experience."

Or get your terminology mixed up: "You're quite a stud. You've scored with a lot of guys." (The fact that this sounds so ridiculous clearly illustrates the double standard.)

Or say, "Well you've certainly lived life to the fullest." Your implication will be clear. Add, "You could write a book some day," implying that your victim is not only loose but indiscreet as well.

"You're smart. You haven't let your body go to waste, the way some girls do. I mean, why go through life as some Vestal Virgin?"

Pretend to be sympathetic. Say, "Listen, I don't think you're a whore. You may have a *slight* reputation—" emphasize the word "slight" as if that mitigates it at all "—but that's just something that's spread around by jealous people and gossipmongers." (What else is a reputation?)

Add, "Anyway, it's not as if you ever did it for money," as if it is only a matter of cash and not numbers that separate her from a street-walker.

"It's not as if you go to bed with just any guy. I mean, there must have been at least one guy you turned down, right?"

"I don't know where you get this reputation for being loose. I mean, it's not as if you've ever participated in a gangbang or anything ... *Have* you?"

When she gets angry, backtrack: "Hey, no offense, all I mean is that you're a woman of the world." (The phrase "man of the world" has positive implications, but no such corresponding phrase exists for women, for the reasons stated above.)

If she remains confrontational, turn the tables, "Who are you kidding, acting so coy? You've been around the block a few times." Gesture at her loin area and comment, "Lotta miles on that odometer."

The Man Who Frequents
Strip Clubs

This pathetic creature is probably married; you can assume his wife doesn't know about his escapades, and if she did, she would probably want to punish him. You're just doing the job for her.

So when your victim suggests the two of you go to a topless bar, respond, "Nah, I don't need to go, I've had plenty of pussy for free in my life."

Ask, in a tone of mild intellectual curiosity, "Tell me, when those girls are giving you a lap dance, trying to cadge a bigger tip from you, what do you think is going through their minds?"

After your victim shrugs, continue. "Do you succumb to the fantasy that these girls are actually attracted to you?"

Your victim will deny this, of course, but continue on in the same vein. "You know, I think that a lot of guys who go to these places actually allow themselves to think that these girls like them. The funny thing is, I've heard that after a girl has worked at a place like that for a while, she grows to really despise her customers."

Your victim will probably shrug as if he doesn't care. Soldier on anyway: "I bet when your favorite girl is giving you a lap dance, she says something to the effect that you're really cute, unlike most of the guys who come in there. But they say that to virtually every guy; it's like a script they're all taught. She's just hoping for a bigger tip."

Your victim will say something to the effect of, "Do you think I don't know that?" But he will squirm nonetheless, because in a little corner of his mind, he has let himself succumb to the fantasy.

Continue, "I've heard that half those strippers are lesbians. If they're not when they start, they turn gay after working in a club for a while. They're surrounded by beautiful women and pathetic guys. Which would you go for? Tough decision."

"Plus nine-tenths of them have had plastic surgery. Do all those implants really turn you on?"

Your victim may say, in semi-humorous fashion, yes, they do. Dampen his joviality with the following observation. "Most of those poor girls must come from broken homes to prostitute themselves like that."

If your victim tries to make the point that they're not really prostitutes, answer, "Of course they are. What do you call getting naked in front of strange guys for money? Anyway, I've heard a lot of them will spend the night with you for five hundred bucks."

If your victim gets angry, respond in kind, "You've seen maybe three pairs of tits for free in your life: one is your wife's, and one is your mother's. You think you're some kind of stud?"

After this, your victim may or may not continue to patronize strip clubs. If he does, he certainly won't ask you to accompany him.

The Unmarried Woman

Any single woman in her thirties who wants to get married is in an awkward position: as desperate as she is, she must not appear that way. This is why many such women often recite a speech about how they're not sure they want to be married, and how they're happy being single.

If your victim is past the age of thirty-five, you can always quote that mythical statistic about how her chances of getting married are less than her chances of being killed by a terrorist.

Unmarried women are constantly trying to prove their popularity. If your victim talks about her many dates, ask, in a tone of exasperated concern, "When is one of these men going to *marry* you?"

If she says that she has been proposed to, just reply, "Sure," in a tone of polite disbelief.

When your victim talks about how she's happy being single, just ignore her and say, in an outraged tone of voice, "Men are so stupid. Look at you. I can't believe you're not married yet. You have so much to *offer* a man. You're smart, you're a good cook, you have your own opinions, you'd be a wonderful mother. So many of these guys can't see past appearances, they all want the same cookie cutter blonde bimbo Stepford wife. Men are such morons! They just don't appreciate a woman with brains."

Ask, "What is the origin of the word spinster? Back in the old days, were unmarried women expected to just sit around and spin a treadle all day?" ("Spinster" is such an old-fashioned word, it may only gradually dawn on your victim that she is one.)

If your victim has a long-time boyfriend who hasn't popped the question yet, ask, "When is he going to make an honest woman out of you?" After your victim tries to brush this off, peer at her closely and revert to that phrase from an earlier era: "You know, nobody's going to buy a cow when milk is free." (It's bad enough when Mom proffers that unwanted advice; for you to do so is downright presumptuous.)

If your victim is living with her boyfriend, say, "Oh, I guess you're happy just to be his mistress then." ("Mistress" is another old-fashioned term few women associate with themselves unless prodded by the likes of you.)

If your victim has other faults, this is a good opportunity to hold them up to the light: "You know, no one is going to marry a girl who smokes/is temperamental/who doesn't cook/who lets herself get so fat."

The Adulterer

The average adulterer thinks of himself as a bad boy rather than a bad man (i.e., naughty rather than evil). After all, what his wife doesn't know won't hurt her, and he's certainly not hurting his kids.

It's up to you to show him he's wrong.

It's most fun to do this when your victim doesn't know that you know he's cheating. If the subject of adultery comes up, let the self-righteousness flow. Say, "No skulking around or tawdry affairs for me. I'd just feel too slimy doing something like that to my family." (Substituting "family" for "wife" insinuates he is hurting his kids as well.)

"Any guy who cheats on his wife is screwing up his children for life. They can always sense when there's something amiss." Shake your head: "Those poor kids."

"I figure if a guy can do that to his own wife, what would he do to his friends?" (Under the standard Guys' Code of Honor, affairs are condoned, but disloyalty to friends is not.)

"Anybody who's cheating on his wife, his wife is probably cheating on him." (Might as well cuckold him while you're at it.)

If your victim goes to church, say, "I plan on going to heaven, not hell." Should your victim try to play devil's advocate here, reply, "People who cheat on their spouses are the lowest form of life on earth. Take Ted Bundy—if he'd been married, he probably would have cheated on his spouse." (As if adultery would have been on a par with his other crimes.)

Conclude, "But I don't even know why I'm saying all this to you. I know you're true blue. In fact, your wife once told me that you may have your other faults, but the one thing that really makes her love you is your fidelity." (It's always nice to hear that your spouse has no real reason to like you.)

If your victim's machismo causes him to see extramarital affairs as a badge of masculine honor, take a different tack. Say, "I'm not one of those guys whose sex drive is so low that after a couple years he loses interest in his wife and needs something new to stimulate him … I feel sorry for those guys who have to cheat. It's as if they all feel they have some inadequacy to make up for."

Add, "Any woman who'd go with a married guy must have a pretty low opinion of herself."

It's most obnoxious to pontificate about adultery if you're a newly-wed, while your victim has been married for over a decade.

If you know whom your victim is cheating with, and she's married, say, "Mr. [Cuckold] told me once that if he ever caught his wife cheating, he'd kill both her and her lover. I believe it, too. He keeps a gun at his house."

If your victim confesses to adultery, which seems highly unlikely given all you've had to say, say very somberly, "That's the first time I've ever been really disappointed in you." (Nobody wants to ruin a perfect record.)

"Your wife would be just devastated if she knew. Don't worry, I'm not going to tell her—even though I probably should." Your victim will probably feel outrage that you would even entertain that thought, but will also realize that he can't offend you too much, or he may just be encouraging you to do so. So he'll have to bite his tongue.

Conclude, "Next time I go to church, I'll say a prayer for you."

The Multiple Divorcee

Men who've been married more than once are usually chagrined mostly about the amount of money they've had to give up. For women, multiple marriages are a sensitive topic because they imply a more personal failure. Make the most of that.

When you find out about your victim's multiple marriages, look at her as if she is a newly discovered species of exotic tropical bug, and exclaim, "Wow! You're a regular Elizabeth Taylor! I've never actually met anyone who's been married three times before. I mean, I've heard of them, and I know they exist, I've just never actually met one."

Add, "I guess you like to collect husbands the way some people collect antique automobiles."

Say, "Tell me, when you have stationery printed up, do you put all your married names at the top (Pamela Digby Churchill Hayward Harriman), or do you just put your current married name? If you do use all your names, do they fit on one line?"

Ask, "Do you ever get confused about which name you are at the moment?"

"Do you measure success in terms of the number of husbands you've had?"

If you've ever met any of her previous husbands, ask, in a spirit of friendly inquiry, "So, how's Tom these days? You guys keep in touch?" as if her ex-husbands are merely old college chums.

Ask, "Are these usually amicable divorces or are they more contentious?" (There is basically no such thing as an "amicable" divorce, despite claims to the contrary.)

"Do you tell each new husband about all the previous ones, or do you say, 'Oh, you're my first!'?"

"You seem to take marriage with the same seriousness that, say, most people take going steady."

"At your weddings, have you changed your vow from 'till death do us part' to 'till the sex cools off'?"

"Maybe next time, you ought to consider just a *friendship* ring or something."

"When you were young, did your mother tell you that marriage is like a game of musical chairs?"

"All those husbands you get, you must be doing something very special for them in bed …"

"How many times do you have to be married before you're officially designated a 'femme fatale'?"

Gay Men

Gay liberation has made great strides in the past couple decades. There are more gay-themed TV shows, and more people are coming out. But not all of the gays have come out, which shows that there is a stigma still attached to homosexuality. Play off this with your gay victim. You mustn't be overtly hostile in any way, merely "unintentionally" insulting.

Start by saying, "You know, some of my best friends are gay." This awkward attempt at friendliness will grate, but will also establish your good intentions. Follow this up with, "Do you like opera?" If his answer is no, ask, "Are you a big Judy Garland fan?"

Wince and ask, in the most sympathetic voice you can muster, "Tell the truth. Doesn't anal sex, uh ... hurt?"

Ask, as if he's never thought of it before, "Aren't you worried about AIDS?"

Plaintively suggest, "You should try girls sometime. Really, you'd like it."

Ask, "Have you ever thought of going to a psychiatrist, getting cured?"

One thing that always drives gays crazy is when they are mistaken for child molesters. Ask, "Have you ever wanted to be, like, a Boy Scout troop leader?"

Ask, "Are you more comfortable in women's clothes or in men's?"

Muse, "I've always wondered, why do they have gay pride parades, but never straight pride parades? And don't you think those parades set the cause back? I mean, I know people who are perfectly accepting of their gay friends; but then they see these guys in their underwear writhing on those floats, and the S&M leather guys all decked out with their butt cheeks showing, and those flamboyant transvestites, and they wonder if maybe they *shouldn't* be so accepting."

Always act as if you think he wants you badly. You may be three hundred pounds and covered in warts, while he looks like a twenty-five-year-old Antonio Banderas. But if he takes a step in your direction, jump back as if from a striking cobra, hold up both palms, and exclaim, "I'm not gay!"

Ask, "Did you ever try to pass as straight? What kinds of things did you say? Did you ever have a beard?"

Then, doubtfully: "Did you ever fool anybody?"

If your victim is a closeted gay, ask him about his girlfriends. Ask for details, like how long he's been going out with her, what it is that attracted him to her, etc. Sooner or later, he will trip himself up, but even if he doesn't, this kind of transparent lying is always fascinating to listen to.

All of these questions and comments should exude well-intentioned curiosity, not mockery. However, if you want to get overtly hostile, when you first see him and he extends his hand for a shake, just wave, as if afraid that even the most casual contact might expose you to HIV. If you really want to be hostile, go ahead and shake his hand—after putting on a latex glove.

Lesbians

Lesbians often (not always, but often) seem to have a chip on their shoulder, especially with men. If you're a man, it is easy to make this chip grow.

Start by sympathizing, "I think it's horrible what AIDS is doing to the gay community." In fact, lesbians are the people least likely to become HIV positive, but it is awkward for her to point this out, as it creates distance from "the cause," so she will probably bite her tongue, always a slightly unpleasant experience.

If she is doing some physical task, ask helpfully, "Need a hand?" This will probably rub her the wrong way. But unless she's very ungracious, she can't very well snap at you, so she'll have to bite her tongue again.

Opine, "You know, I get the impression that the reason a lot of women become lesbians is because no man wants them." Hastily add, "Not that they're not better off with a woman," to prevent her from biting your head off. (By this point, her tongue should be a bloody mess.)

Say, "I prefer women myself," as if this makes the two of you simpatico.

If your victim is at all masculine, say, "I bet lipstick lesbians are in big demand by the bull dykes. But you know what? I bet those lipstick lezzies prefer each other. I sure know which type I'd prefer."

Talk to her as if she's one of the guys. Nudge her with your elbow and say, "Hey, how about that Keira Knightley, huh? I bet you'd like to get your hands on *that*."

Assume she is the living embodiment of every lesbian stereotype: "I bet you just love softball."

Any attempt to "relate" to her on these terms will ring terminally hollow. Say, "Hey, how about the New York Liberty, eh?" (The number of heterosexual men nationwide who are women's professional basketball fans can probably be counted on the fingers of one hand.)

"I thought Sappho was a great poet."

"I really enjoyed that movie *Fried Green Tomatoes*." After each comment, look as if you expect to be applauded.

The best way to rile her is to talk about your own, completely chauvinistic relationship with your wife or girlfriend. Say, "Personally, I like to come home and have my wife meet me at the door with a martini in her hand. Then I sit down in my easy chair and she massages my feet for a while. If she doesn't do a good job, I spank her. And you know what? She likes it that way."

When your lesbian victim expresses outrage at this arrangement, lash back: "Hey, I don't criticize your lifestyle! Why do you criticize mine? I thought that gays believed that what happens in the privacy of your own house between consenting adults was nobody else's business!"

If He Thinks He's a Stud

If you're a woman who's just gone to bed with a guy, and he's acting obnoxious (post-coitus, the salesmanship tends to stop, and the real personality tends to emerge), you're in the perfect position to take your victim down a peg or two.

After sex, many guys will start fishing for a favorable review of their sexual prowess. Give him the opposite.

If your victim asks if you had an orgasm, just say, "Oh, it's not important." He will then say something to the effect of, "Well, did you at least enjoy it?" Smile inscrutably and give him those four damning words: "You're a nice guy."

Ask, "Was that you first time?" After he strenuously denies this, follow up with, "Have there been many others?"

When he asks if he really seems that inexperienced, shrug, "It's just that I've been with experts."

Ask politely, "Have you ever given a woman an orgasm?" After he emphatically says yes, quickly reply, "Okay, okay, no need to get sensitive."

If he asks you for pointers, reply, as if he's asked you something ridiculous, "I can't teach you how to make love to a woman! You should read a book or something."

If he's really a jerk, and you have absolutely no desire to see him again, as soon as he finishes, ask incredulously, "Is that all you're going to do to me?" After he expresses bewilderment, snap, "I guess you don't care about a woman's pleasure."

Then ask, cryptically, "Do you mind?" When he asks you what you mean, start to masturbate. Close your eyes, fake an orgasm, then breathe a big contented sigh. Explain, "Sorry, but I need satisfaction too." Then ask, "Have you always had a problem with endurance?"

If your victim has been totally impotent, he probably won't act obnoxious afterwards, but you may have decided by this point that you dislike him anyway. He's already embarrassed, so you don't have to say much. Just muse, "I'd heard that there are impotent guys out there." This is a double-edged barb: First, it classifies him as an "impotent guy," as if this is a permanent condition. Second, it implies that you've never run across one before yourself, which isolates him in his impotence.

Twist the sword a little: "You know, there's no shame in taking Viagra, even at your age." (This line is even more effective if he actually did perform.) Say, "Well, it's just something to think about."

PART IV
Personality Types

The Temperamental Twit

If you use the techniques in this book, sooner or later your victim will fly into a rage. Rather than acquiesce in the face of his rage, or continue to argue your point, draw attention to his emotional state.

Make the sound of a foghorn—as best you can—and announce, "Fragile ego alert! Fragile ego alert! Handle with care! Use kid gloves!"

Or calmly observe, "You're the most temperamental person I know."

Tut-tut, "Some people have the emotional maturity of six-year-olds."

"I guess self-control isn't your strong suit."

"You know, irritability is a sign of low character."

"It's got to be tough going through life with your nerves on edge all the time."

Ask, "Do you always throw a tantrum when you don't get your way?"

"Did you know that people have strokes when they're throwing tantrums like this? Have you had your blood pressure checked recently?"

If you can manage to laugh in the face of his anger, do so and say, "Look at you! Your face is all red!" This will send him through the roof.

If your victim is a woman, ask, "Whatsamatter, forget your broomstick today? You're lucky you weren't around in Salem in 1693 ... If I poured a bucket of water on you, would you start screaming, 'I'm melting! Curses, I'm melting!'?"

Or suggest that her anger has a different derivation. Just say, "Why don't you buy yourself a new set of batteries?" She'll probably get your drift, but if she doesn't, explain, "For your vibrator."

The Drama Queen

Unfortunately, it is impossible to curb a drama queen's histrionics in any permanent way, but there are ways to tone down his behavior in the short run.

Ask, "Have you always been such a drama queen?" Use of the word "queen" with a male should have an inhibiting effect on him. The phrase "Don't get your panties in a twist" will send the same message.

Say, "Your life is one big soap opera. One emotion-packed scene after another. Don't you ever feel like taking a break?"

"Every little problem that arises, you react as if the sky is falling down. What do you do when there's a real emergency?"

At the next outburst, ask, "Exactly why is the sky falling down this time?"

If you think he remembers his nursery tales, ask, "Which one are you, Chicken Little or Henny Penny?"

"It must be very tiring getting hysterical all the time. Seriously, it looks as if it consumes a lot of energy. You should learn to relax."

"Does your doctor not prescribe Valium?"

Try sarcasm: "What I've always admired most about you is that no matter the situation, you stay unruffled."

Or call someone else over: "Hey Joey, come on over here—you gotta see this. Billy is having another hissy fit. He's putting on a great show."

Often the drama queen is in a fury against some third person over some perceived slight or injustice. As he recounts to you what gall and hypocrisy this third person showed, take the other person's side. Say, "Look at it from his viewpoint," then calmly proceed to do so. This is

pouring gasoline on a fire—there's something very satisfying about seeing those flames shoot ever higher.

The Pollyanna

We've all known the overly cheerful person who whitewashes everything, and thus goes through life an incurable optimist. It's up to you to inform him how incredibly annoying he is.

"Are you always this cheerful, or is this a special occasion?"

"Did you just win the lottery?"

"Seriously, what do you have to be so happy about?"

"Why are you so bubbly all the time?" Your victim will probably give you an answer to the effect of, he just decided to be that way, since he only has one life to live, etc. In fact, temperament seems to be mostly a matter of neurochemistry, but those people whose dial is set permanently to "happy" always feel obliged to justify it with some philosophical twaddle, as if their temperaments were arrived at via conscious decision. Respond, "You know, I don't think you could be really sad if you wanted to."

"Is there anything that makes you morose?"

"How would you feel if a close friend died? Sad? Or would you just go bouncing through the funeral the way you do through the rest of your life?"

Point at a glass filled halfway, and ask, "How would you describe that glass?"

Ask, "Why are cheerful people always so corny?"

"I guess you're what they call a chirpy twerpy."

Or, sarcastically, "You've got to change your dark, pessimistic attitude towards life. You should try to be happier. Really, the world can be a very nice place if you let it. Remember, smile and the world smiles with you."

After all this, he may tone it down a little. But it's unlikely.

The Ass-Kisser

A certain amount of ass-kissing is inevitable in life if you're not independently wealthy. People who do this usually think of it as an unpleasantness they must perform occasionally for business reasons. Your job is to convince your victim it goes much deeper than that, right down to the essence of his soul.

If you witness your victim in his subservient role, spell out the shameful nature of his abasement.

First, act surprised: "Wow. That sort of stuff just comes naturally to you, doesn't it?"

When your victim asks what you mean, reply, "Being a lackey. I actually thought you were too much of a man to act like that."

"Don't you find having to grovel a little humiliating?"

"I honestly thought you had more self-respect."

If your victim says he has to act that way because of his job, ask, "So what's the worm's eye view like around here?"

"When your boss makes a stupid, lame joke, do you laugh really hard?"

Ask, "Don't you ever feel unclean after you act that way? Like you need a shower or something?"

"Does your boss actually enjoy being blown like that or is he sort of disgusted?"

Ask, "Need some?" and hand him some ChapStick.

Offer to get him some kneepads.

Take a tissue and dab at the tip of his nose, saying, "I just wanted to wipe some of the brown off."

Or, more directly, "So, how does his behind taste?"

Conclude, "Oh well, I guess some people just gravitate towards ass-kissing. It's a question of character."

The Hypochondriac

If your victim is a hypochondriac, the best way to reach him is by asking, "Are you okay?" When he asks why you ask, reply, "You don't look well, that's all." This should set in motion a whole train of worries sure to make his mood spiral down. Ask as if you are seriously concerned for his health, and it won't occur to him that you are mocking him.

Offer, "Lot of bad germs going around right now." (This is always the case.)

Say, "Lotta people seem to have the flu." Add ominously, "And worse."

Explain, "The problem with germs is, you can never see them. But they're everywhere. On restaurant tables. On doorknobs. In the air we breathe. One thing's for sure—I don't like to shake people's hands."

If he's drinking coffee, remind him, "Caffeine is a vasoconstrictor, you know. Makes you more prone to strokes."

If he's savoring rich food, comment, "That stuff will give you a heart attack. The fats congeal both in and *around* the arteries, giving you arteriosclerosis *and* athlerosclerosis."

If anyone is smoking nearby, say, "That secondhand smoke can kill you. I can just *feel* my alveoli closing up when I'm around a smoker."

If he's enjoying a glass of wine, say, "Making your liver work overtime, eh? Cirrhosis is a horrible way to go."

If it's hazy outside, sniff the air and say, "Pollution's really bad today. Can you smell it?" He may not be able to, but will imagine that he can. Add, "I'm thinking about getting one of those gauze masks, just so I don't have to breathe all this garbage in. This stuff will really make you sick." (The reverse placebo effect usually works quite effectively with hypochondriacs.)

If it's a beautiful day and the sun is shining, tell your victim, "Now that the ozone layer's been depleted, a lot more people are getting melanoma."

No matter what kind of fun he's having, you can pretty much kill it. Even if he's sitting inside just reading a book without any caffeine, alcohol, smoke, or ultraviolet rays, tell him, "I don't think the light's good in here. Keep reading like that and your eyes are going to go, you know."

You can wipe the very smile right off his face by looking carefully at his teeth and asking, "You flossing every day? You gotta be careful; I hear those dentures can be a real pain."

If the hypochondriac drones on without encouragement about his various maladies, the best way to cut him dead is simply to ask, "Are you a hypochondriac?" This is one of those trick questions, like "Are you modest," which is impossible to answer truthfully. (A true hypo really thinks he's sick, or at least surrounded by very real threats to his health.)

Inform him, "The only kind of doctor you need is a shrink." This may start him worrying about psychological as well as physical maladies.

Torturing the hypochondriac is so easy it seems almost unsporting.

The Neurotic

A neurotic invents reasons to suffer when there aren't any. If your victim is a neurotic, it's easy to make him suffer even more.

First, suggest the impossible: "Just relax. I don't know why you're so uptight all the time. Chill, man."

Act totally mystified by his fears: "All you have to do is give a speech? What are you so worried about? All you have to do is talk. You talk to me all the time. That doesn't seem to bother you."

Neurotics always worry about being "different" than others, so you also want to make your victim feel as much like an alien as possible: "Geez, you're the only person I've ever known who worries about such silly little things ... I never *heard* of anyone so fretful."

Once you've established that your victim is a complete freak, reassure him, "Don't worry, there's nothing wrong with being a little different." If he seems to take solace from this, add, "But being a *lot* different, that's another matter."

Neurotics tend to plan ahead, so be sure to comment on this aspect of his life: "Are you always this regimented? You must just hate freedom!"

Point out, "You're very self-destructive, aren't you?" Don't provide any specifics; just the suggestion will suffice to set him off on a worrying jag.

Play amateur psychologist. No one other than the neurotic would pay attention to this type of silliness, but he is vulnerable:

"Do you wash your hands a lot, that sort of thing?"

"Do you have problems with sex? You strike me as the type who might have potency issues."

"Have you ever considered getting professional help? It's nothing to be ashamed of; really, plenty of people do it."

Interpret your victim's neatness in a Freudian light: "Wow, are you ever anal!" (This charge is impossible to disprove.) Ask, "Did your mother toilet train you forcibly when you were small?" (Who remembers that?)

If you are at his house, open his desk drawer and say, "Man, are you ever a neat freak! Look at the way you have those pencils all lined up and sharpened, ready to go."

Say, "Oh look, the fringes on that rug aren't straight. Doesn't that just drive you crazy?" Nudge the fringes with your foot to mess them up further, then look at him expectantly, as if you expect him to drop to his knees and straighten them out feverishly.

Tell your victim, "You have obsessive-compulsive disorder. You do. You have all the hallmarks. Ted Bundy had it too, you know." (Bundy, like most sociopaths, was the opposite of a neurotic, but most people wouldn't know this.) Obsessive-compulsive disorder has received enough publicity recently that your victim is probably aware of it, and may consider himself a candidate. If you confirm it for him, it will at least sow a seed of self-doubt.

Accuse Him of Being
a Sociopath

If your victim accuses you of being neurotic, shoot back that he is a sociopath. It's possible to accuse practically anybody of sociopathy, in much the same way it is possible to see anybody in the description of every astrological sign. If you know your victim well enough, you can come up with an example of his behavior to illustrate virtually every facet of sociopathy.

Start by saying matter-of-factly, "You know, you have a lot of the traits of sociopathy." After he denies it, recite the following list:

"First of all, you're very relaxed—just like a sociopath." (We *all* relax at times.)

"You're very impulsive." (We're all impulsive at times.)

"You're dishonest." (Who among us has never lied?)

"You're a risk taker." (If he asks for proof, mention the last time he drove through a yellow light.)

"You're a backstabber." (We all criticize others behind their backs more than we do to their faces.)

"You're incapable of real love." (How does one prove one is?)

"You're awfully egotistical." (Everybody has an ego.)

"You're awfully egocentric." (Everybody is selfish.)

If your victim ever displays any of the above characteristics, use this as confirmation: "Uh-huh, once a sociopath always a sociopath."

Ask, "What did you think of Ted Bundy," as if you think he might give himself away by blurting out, "Oh, I really liked him!"

In case he doesn't get your point, ask, "Have you ever had the urge to go out and kill a lot of people, one by one?"

Keep in mind, if your victim actually *is* a sociopath, and doesn't want word of this leaking out, he may just decide to slice you up and have you for breakfast.

The Liar

Everybody lies when they have to. But only scoundrels lie when they don't have to. (People who lie about their own exploits are a particularly low breed.) After extended contact, it will always become apparent that somebody is less than honest. You'll never cure a chronic liar, but you can at least call him on his tendency.

Ask him, "Do you think the phrase 'pathological liar' applies to you?" When your victim denies it, answer dismissively, "Of course, that's exactly what a pathological liar would say."

Next time he lies, ask him, "Did you ever hear the story of 'The Boy Who Cried Wolf'?" When he says yes, just nod and look off into the distance.

Say, "I guess everybody has to make a decision early on with you—whether to believe their eyes or their ears."

"Do people ask you to take lie detector tests very often?"

"You seem to have a little bit of a credibility issue."

After the next whopper, look down and examine his legs closely. When he asks what you're doing, reply, "Just checking to see if your pants were on fire. You have heard that expression, haven't you?"

Ask, "Do you always just say whatever comes to mind at the moment, whatever people might want to hear? Is that how your mind works?"

Sociopaths (who are by definition utterly dishonest, amoral creatures) sometimes like to say that they were in the Special Forces or the CIA, even if they weren't. If your victim claims any such farfetched tale of glory, don't call him a liar. Just keep asking him questions about it. Eventually he will trip himself up with conflicting stories. Let him talk long enough, and he will dig a hole, jump in it, and even start throwing dirt on himself. Wait until he does that, and then point at some of his inconsistencies.

The Bully

The best way to get back at a bully is not to respond to his individual taunts, but to call him on his character.

Start by asking, "Are you a sociopath?" (Scratch a bully and you'll almost inevitably find a sociopath; of course, being such, he will lie about it.)

"Why is it that you love to pick on people so much?" Ask in a spirit of honest intellectual inquiry, as if you're genuinely curious what makes him the way he is.

"Why don't you ever pick on [someone with the power to hurt him]?"

"Is it true what they say about bullies? That when someone pushes them back, they'll show you what cowards they are?"

"Does picking on someone who is smaller and weaker than you make you feel big and strong?"

"Don't you ever wonder why everybody hates you so much?" (This will give even the most thick-skinned pause, and will devastate the thin-skinned.)

"Did your father pick on you when you were young? Is that where you learned to act like this?"

Ask innocently, "What was your mother like when you were growing up—warm and tender and loving?" (Most bullies had mothers who just went through the motions.)

Ask a bully about his parents, and you'll be sure to find a scab you can pick at.

Pick at it long enough, and you may even get him to erupt in a torrent of self-pity, after which he will have a hard time bullying you again. (If he does, just say, "Come on, *you* didn't like it when your parents acted this way to *you*.")

The Second-Guesser

If you know someone who likes to tell people what they did wrong after the fact, by definition that person deserves to be your victim. Feel free to use every other insult in the book with him, but start by letting him know how useless his advice is.

After he second-guesses you for the umpteenth time, ask, "Do you think the phrase 'Monday morning quarterback' applies to you? Cause if there's a Super Bowl for Monday morning quarterbacking, you should definitely be in it."

If he does it again, marvel, "Wow. You're a Tuesday and Wednesday morning quarterback as well."

"Next time, instead of telling me what I should have done yesterday, tell me what I should do tomorrow. It's more helpful."

"You know how they say hindsight is twenty-twenty? You have the vision of an eagle."

"You're a reverse Cassandra—you're very good at foretelling the past."

Or just turn the tables. If your victim stubs his toe, suggest, "You shouldn't do that." Laugh and say, "See? My advice is as helpful as yours."

Mr./Mrs. Cute

If your victim tries to act cute, it is your sacred duty to cure him of this behavior. The best way is to throw up and then explain why you did so. But if you can't vomit on command, just ask, "Do you actually think you're being cute when you do that?" After your victim gives some noncommittal, backtracking kind of reply, raise your eyebrows, close your eyes, and give a quick shake of your head, as if you can't quite believe that anyone at his age would still be trying to act cute.

Explain, "Children about four or five years of age are cute when they make mistakes. By the time they're seven or eight, if they try to act cute, they've usually lost it. By ten, it's completely gone. *Grownups* who try …" Shake your head and let your conclusion go unspoken.

If your victim continues to show symptoms of the Cute Disease, say, "I think your diapers need changing. There's a very bad smell coming from your general vicinity, that of an adult acting like a four-year-old."

Ask, stone-faced, "How do other people respond to your act? Do they give you an indulgent smile and say, 'Aww, he's so cute'?"

If your victim responds that you need to loosen up, reply, "I'm loose enough. I think you need to tighten up some."

Comment, "I guess you're going through your childhood now. Pretty soon, you'll be going through your teenage years, where you use bad words and drink beer to be cool. All I ask is fair warning when puberty approaches."

Or postulate your Theory of Cuteness: "I think adults who try to act cute do so because they didn't get enough affection from their parents and are forever after trying to make up for it."

The best way to kill the undesired behavior, however, is actually to encourage him. Whenever he is not in the mood to act cute, ask him to. Say, "Hey, can you act cute for me? I love it when you do that. Go ahead. Say something cute. Please? Come on." If he does ever again try to act cute, call some others over and ask him to repeat his act for them, telling them, "He is so cute. You've just got to see this." This should have a nicely chilling effect.

The Egocentrist

This creature is always a trial. If you can point out his egocentrism to him, you may be able to get him to be a touch less selfish, if only on a temporary basis.

Start by observing, "Galileo was wrong." When your victim asks what you mean, explain, "The world doesn't revolve around the sun. It revolves around you."

"It *is* all about you."

"You're the kind of guy who'd have his own website—as if anyone would be interested in reading about the details of your life."

"Do you sometimes think that other people are robots who were put here merely for your convenience?"

"You must find it incredibly annoying when others occasionally want to have their way."

"Were you the kind of child who would say, 'It's my ball and if you don't let me win, I'm going to take it home'?"

"If there was an earthquake and thousands of homes were destroyed, including yours, would you think, 'Why was God out to get me?'"

If you go to a movie with him, say, "It was nice of the studio to make this movie for you."

In a traffic jam, "All these people stuck here just to inconvenience you."

Tell your victim, "We're all the star of the movie that is our life, but you're *really* the star."

PART V

Vices and Other Weaknesses

The Smoker

Every smoker knows the risks he is incurring. And no smoker needs to be reminded of these concerns. Unless, of course, he is your victim.

Start by asking your victim if he's addicted. Use the terms that apply to other types of junkies: "How often do you need a fix? Do you go through withdrawal? Do you shake and have hallucinations, or just get really edgy? Have you ever thought of checking into a rehab center?"

Ask your victim if he has tried a nicotine patch. After he confesses that they just didn't seem to work with him, tell him, "You know, all you have to do is just stop smoking. It's just a matter of will power." (There is nothing more annoying to an addict than to have a non-addict tell him how easy it is to give up his habit.)

After your victim tells you how hard it is to quit, just shrug and comment, "Oh well. If you gave up smoking, you'd probably just gain twenty pounds anyway."

Inform him, "You know, smoking lowers the body's natural immune system. It's sort of like having voluntary AIDS."

Shudder and say, "I was in a museum once that showed what the inside of a smoker's lung looked like. Grossest thing I ever saw. Like a piece of charcoal, all blackened and useless. I just can't imagine doing that to myself."

Say, "I hope you don't smoke around your children. You'd be killing them. Nobody who loves his children would ever do that." This will cause him to guiltily recall the few times he allowed his children to be within the presence of his smoke.

Ask, "Have you ever listened to one of those guys who've had throat cancer talk after having his vocal cords removed? Who has to press one of those little contraptions against his throat so he sounds like an electronic kazoo?" Laugh as if you find this funny.

If the health hazards don't bother your victim, try reaching him through his vanity: "Ever notice how smokers always look around ten years older than they actually are? Their skin always gets that grayish, wrinkled quality."

Add, "I've heard that smokers often become impotent too."

Say, "I'm so glad smoking has been banned inside offices and airplanes and bars now."

Muse, "As far as I'm concerned, they should put a twenty-dollar tax on every pack. Heck, they should probably just outlaw it, the way they do other destructive drugs."

Give your victim an inquisitive look and ask, "Do you think smoking makes you cool?" Then do an imitation of a smoker trying to look sophisticated.

Say, "I would never kiss a girl who smokes. They taste horrible. You can just smell the nicotine coming through their every pore. Yecch."

It is the rare smoker nowadays who is rude enough to smoke in an enclosed space with nonsmokers present. Most will leave a building to have their cigarette. So follow your victim outside, and badger him there.

The Moderate Social Drinker

Should your victim happen to be a moderate drinker, ask him, "You ever think about joining AA?"

Your victim will laughingly tell you that he is not an alcoholic. Reply, "Admitting your problem is the first step on the road to recovery. If you can't do that, you're really in trouble."

Your victim will then strenuously deny having a problem with alcohol. Reply, "They say if you have just one drink a day, you're an alcoholic. And I've seen you have more than one."

Your victim may lose his temper. Nod as if this is the reaction you expected, and say, "See? The very vehemence of your response shows how much you have to hide. It's practically an admission of guilt." If he gets even angrier, say, "Hmm. The problem is more deep-seated than I thought."

When he says that you're being utterly ridiculous, take a deep breath, as if about to confide something—only very reluctantly. "You know, I've already spoken to your parents about this, and we agree. You really should join AA."

After he expresses outrage at this invasion of his privacy, return his fire: "Hey! You're way out of line! I'm only trying to help you! This is how you thank me? I just don't want you to end up as some Skid Row bum, that's all."

Arrange with several of his friends to have an intervention. A good time is guaranteed for all—all except your victim. When confronted thusly, he will groan and ask if you are all really serious. Insist you are. You just have to make sure everybody keeps a straight face.

The longer you're able to keep up this charade, the more fun you'll have. (If you don't think you're capable of keeping a straight face, it helps to have a few drinks beforehand.)

The Recovering Alcoholic

If your victim has had a problem with alcohol in the past, he is one of the easiest people in the world to torture. Just follow this simple twelve-step program:

First, if he doesn't realize that you know he is an alcoholic, invite him to a bar. If he does know, or if he informs you when you invite him, ask him to a restaurant with a liquor license instead.

Second, before you order a drink, ask him if it will bother him that you're drinking. Almost every alcoholic will tell you not to be silly, to go right ahead. (Most are eager to demonstrate that they have things under control.)

Third, when the waiter comes, rather than ask about the food, inquire as to what drinks are available. If the waiter says, whatever you like, ask him to name a few drinks and then ask what their ingredients are.

Fourth, mull over your choices at length, then order your usual drink.

Fifth, when your beer arrives, take a big gulp, then let out a deep, satisfied sigh, as if you have just tasted the best thing on earth (which, in his mind, you just have). Lick your lips as if to savor every last drop.

Sixth, set your glass down halfway between the two of you, so that the smell of your drink wafts over. Propose frequent toasts to which he will have to raise his water glass; this underscores his inability to have a real drink.

Seventh, start the conversation by asking about his alcoholism. (Every alcoholic has a story to tell.)

Eighth, while he is telling his tale of woe, drink up. Act fascinated, but giggle at inappropriate moments, as if you find the very concept of alcoholism funny.

Ninth, about halfway through his story, when he gets to the part about how he lost control of his life, shake your head and say, "I guess some people just can't handle alcohol," as if such weakness is beyond your comprehension. As he continues, cluck, "I just can't imagine letting myself get like that."

Tenth, when he warns you—as you order drink after drink—that you may be on the slippery slope yourself, say, slightly contemptuously, "Don't worry, I'm not like you; I can handle it."

Eleventh, when your victim gets to the end of his story, the part where he joined AA and found salvation and hasn't had a drink in three hundred and forty-seven days, look at your watch and say, "Yup, it's been about fifteen seconds for me." Then take another gulp and say, "Oops, better make that one second." If you're not too tipsy, stand up at the table and announce, "My name is Nick Casanova and I'm an alcoholic," then collapse in laughter as if you've just done something really clever.

Twelfth, as the evening wears on, after he has enviously watched you drink yourself into euphoria, order a large drink, set it halfway between the two of you, and go to the men's room. The entire time you're away, that glass will be whispering, "Drink me, drink me," to him with a seductive power no woman could ever exert.

Follow these steps and you will drop your victim like a bad habit.

The Talkaholic

Yelling "Shut up!" at a nonstop talker has an appealing directness, but is too confrontational for most of us. Better to ask, in your most polite voice, "Listen, I don't mean to be rude or anything, but could you please talk just a little less?" Ask reluctantly, as if you've been forced to your limits and have no choice but to make the request. The politer you are, the more bite your plea will have.

Or ask, in a very tired voice, "Precisely how do you expect me to use that piece of information?" Keep pressing until it is clear you want to be burdened with no more useless trivia.

If you ask your victim a question, end it by wincingly adding, "In twenty-five words or less, *please*."

If he's telling a long-winded story, interrupt with, "Is there an end to this, or does it just go on forever? My ears are really getting sore."

Spontaneously break out into that song from the sixties, "Silence is golden, golden …"

Pretend to fall asleep. Put your head in your arms, close your eyes, and snore.

Ask, "Seriously, don't your vocal cords ever get tired? You have to be careful, you could develop a polyp or something."

"What happens when you get laryngitis?"

Pull open your victim's jacket and look around inside, as if trying to locate something. When he asks what you're doing, reply, "I'm looking for the off button."

Or ask, "How do I turn the volume down?"

"Anybody have any duct tape?"

"If your home was invaded, and you were hiding in your closet, and you didn't want the intruder to find you, because you knew he wanted to murder you, would you be able to keep quiet then or would you have to just keep talking?"

Ask, "All that talking, do you ever have time to think?"

Or just tell your victim, "Listen, from now on I want you just to pretend I'm deaf." After that, if he says anything, just cup your hand around your ear as a deaf person would and shrug, indicating that it is useless to talk to you.

Or be sympathetic. Ask, "You really hate silence, don't you? It must somehow be really scary for you to have to fill it up all the time. Do you feel that a breath without a vocalization is a wasted breath? Have you ever considered joining TA?"

When he asks what TA is, reply, "Talkaholics Anonymous. It's sort of like one of those Quaker meetings—you just sit and have an hour of silence. Think you could handle that?" Look at him appraisingly, then shake your head no.

Mock Someone Else with the Same Achilles' Heel

Mocking your victim for his weaknesses will make him angry and he will respond in kind. But making fun of someone else with the same weaknesses will make him feel ashamed and embarrassed instead.

If your victim suffers from obesity, talk about a third party's weight problem as if it is a personal affront to you. ("That sow must never take the feedbag off. Ugh. You'd think she'd have a little self-control.")

If your victim is spindly, dwell on that. ("That pencil-neck geek Richard oughta go on steroids or something. You'd think he'd be embarrassed to be seen like that.")

If he has acne, make the most of somebody else's zits. ("I swear, I can't eat when I'm in the same room as him. It nauseates me, it really does.")

If your victim is ugly, give the same treatment. ("Joanne's looking good—I guess she forgot her broomstick today.")

If your victim is insecure about his intelligence, rant about a mutual acquaintance's stupidity. ("I swear, there's no way Jimmy's IQ is triple digits. Dumb people ought to just be shot and put out of their misery.")

If you happen to know your victim hasn't had sex in a long time, ridicule someone else for his lack of a sex life. ("I don't think Joey could get laid if he was the Good Humor man in a town full of starving prostitutes.")

If your victim likes his coffee, scoff at that. ("Jack can't even function in the morning unless he gets his daily fix of coffee. You know, people who need their caffeine are no better than heroin addicts.")

If your victim likes to drink, make your feelings about that vice clear. ("Ever notice how liquor makes people incredibly stupid? You know, Sam probably gets drunk every week. He's an alcoholic in the making.")

At some point, your victim will admit, guiltily, that he has the same problem. Reassure him, "Oh no you don't." Then add bitterly, "But Sam does. What a contemptible piece of crap."

In short, if your victim has a physical flaw, talk about that flaw as if it's a character fault. If your victim has a character fault, place it on a par with child molesting.

Laud a Trait Your Victim Lacks

One way to strike a nice deep chord of insecurity in your victim is to lavish praise on someone else for a quality your victim does not have.

If your victim is a non-athlete, praise a star athlete to the skies. Make it sound as if he has done everyone a great favor by coming down from Mount Olympus to associate with them. Effuse about how girls will do anything to get him into bed because he is such a great athlete.

If your victim is insecure about his looks, rave about the looks of a mutual acquaintance. Talk about how "the face one presents to the world" is the most important quality a person has.

If your victim is insecure about the size of his penis, talk about a friend of yours whom women absolutely adore. When your victim asks why women adore him so, reply, "What do you think? He's well hung"—as if you're surprised he would even ask such a silly question. Say that once his reputation gets around among the ladies, they just pass him along from one to the next. If your victim has the temerity to venture that he's heard that penis size doesn't matter that much, say you've talked to girls who laugh and say, "Right, women don't care about a man's penis size any more than men care about a woman's looks."

The virtue you choose to praise, of course, need not be a personal trait. It can be anything your victim lacks—a nice car, a nice house, a tidy bank account.

By the time you are through, your victim should be thoroughly depressed.

You must be careful, however, about raving too much about your friend's athletic ability, looks, and especially genitalia if you're a man who does not want to appear gay.

Fear of Flying

If you ever saw *A Clockwork Orange*, you may remember the scene in which the antihero, Alex, is subjected to the Ludovico technique: he is made to feel chemically induced nausea while being forced to watch some of his favorite activities (i.e., rape and mayhem). Once he is negatively conditioned like that, he is no longer able to indulge in these activities, and thus, from society's standpoint, he is cured.

If your victim has a fear of flying, you can use the same type of operant conditioning to cure him of his predilection for hanging around you. If you know his phobia, poke at it, prod it, even expose him to it. Do everything you can to associate that horror with you.

If you're in a plane together, you can have a lot of fun. If it's raining, point out, "You know, your chances of crashing are four hundred times greater in a thunderstorm."

Once the plane is airborne, stamp on the floor as hard as you can, and say, "This plane doesn't really seem that sturdy to me."

When the flight attendant demonstrates how to use the oxygen mask, confide in your victim, "Are you kidding me? This thing goes down, they'll find our bodies in ten separate pieces. But hey—at least they'll be well oxygenated!"

Point at the wings and observe that they seem to be bending, as if not firmly attached to the fuselage. Comment, "Sure hope this plane doesn't have metal fatigue." When the fasten seat belt light goes on, observe, "Don't worry, these'll save us. All those plane crashes you hear about where everybody was killed? That's because they weren't wearing their seat belts!"

After provoking his fear, helpfully suggest, "Sometimes I think your problems are all in your own head."

If you experience turbulence, look at your victim and say excitedly, "I love turbulence! It's like surfing the big one at Waimea!" Then cry, "We're going down! We're going down!" Reach over, feel his palms, and comment laughingly, "A little sweaty, eh?" Place your fingertips on his wrist and take his pulse. Then turn sympathetic: "Oh hell, I don't blame you for being scared; people die from crashes regularly."

Eventually, your victim should get that queasy phobic feeling just by looking at you.

"Oh—That's So Sad"

If you really want to drive your victim to drink, pretend to sympathize with some aspect of his life he may not previously have regarded as pathetic. Even if your victim is a two-fisted, steam-coming-out-of-his-ears Type A, do your best to turn him into a sad sack.

If he went to see a movie by himself, say, in the most sympathetic voice you can muster, "You went to see a movie by yourself? That's the saddest thing I ever heard."

Turn any situation into an occasion for sadness. "She didn't want to see you again after the first date? That's so sad." Say it with all the tremulous pathos you can, so that your victim can almost hear violins in the background.

Add, "I don't understand why people don't like you. You seem nice to me."

Under the guise of false sympathy, you can get away with all sorts of insults:

"You make only thirty-five thousand a year? That's so sad …"

"You ate at McDonald's? That's so sad."

"This is where you live? This is so sad."

"You have to drive an hour to and from work every day? That's so sad."

"This is your car?" You know the drill.

Make sure your victim is aware that you are speaking from a position of superiority. The subtext of your sympathy is always, "You're so weak, so dumb, so poor, so ineffectual, so unpopular …"

Conclude, "You lead a hard, lonely life. It must be tough."

Self-pity is not the most unpleasant of emotions, but it is a poor substitute for pride. If you are good at this technique, you can make your victim's pride evaporate. If you're very good, you can make him feel like Job.

The Dog Lover

The old dictum is often true: a dog may actually be his owner's best friend. So an insult to the dog will often be taken personally by its owner. If your victim has a dog, take advantage of this.

Start by insulting its breed. Let's say your friend has a Golden Retriever. Casually opine, "I had a friend who had a Golden Retriever, and it ran smack dab into a car and got killed. He said afterward he didn't really miss it though because it was so dumb. I hear they're all supposed to be that way."

"There's a reason you never see Golden Retrievers as Seeing Eye dogs or rescue dogs. They use the intelligent breeds for those jobs. Golden Retrievers have a hard time with 'sit' and 'stay' and 'roll over'."

"You know, another thing about Golden Retrievers is that they're pretty weak for their size. Any terrier half its size could beat one in a fight." (Even the most committed pacifist takes pride in his dog's athleticism, so your victim should bridle.) If he argues, suggest, "Then you should try putting him in a fight sometime. They have organized ones in the barrio."

Say, "Golden Retrievers are really slow. My friend who had one—whenever his cat got mad at it, it would chase after him and rake his hindquarters. That dog just could never get away."

"The friend said that his dog, which was a female, had a litter and then ate most of her babies. He said he was shocked, but when he talked to other Golden Retriever owners, they said that they found the same thing, that they ate their own young."

Say, "It really gives off a strong dog smell, doesn't it?" If the owner disagrees, say, "I guess you just don't smell it anymore." (To the owner, his dog is always a "he" or a "she"; to you, it's an "it.")

If you're in your victim's house, sniff and observe, "Smells like a pet shop in here."

Hold up your victim's dog by his hind legs and spread them wide, peering closely at its crotch: "Did you have him spayed?" (Most male dogs are.) If the answer is yes, wince and ask, "If you have a son, are you going to castrate him so he'll be less trouble too?" If your victim hasn't had his dog spayed, ask, "So does he hump your leg all the time?"

Before you let the dog down, cry, "Wheelbarrow!" and make it walk on its front legs.

Ask, "Is it my imagination or is Lassie here walking with a limp? A lot of dogs develop hip problems you know." (Your victim will tell you his dog's name, but pay no heed; refer to it as "Toto" or "Rex" or "Lassie.")

Dogs are like children—their owners always see them as beautiful. So say, "That thing really looks like a flea bag. You should consider having it groomed. Nah, nothing would help that dog. Man, is he ugly!"

Say all these things matter-of-factly, not as if you're *trying* to insult the dog. As personally as your victim will take all these insults, he knows that he must not appear to be taking them hard or he will appear foolish.

Ask, "How old is it?" If the dog is eight or older, wave a hand dismissively. "Oh—no wonder he's so decrepit."

Ask, "When you're away, what does it do, just sit around and wait for you? Oh well, it's a dog's life."

"You know, they say if you turn a dog over on its back and tickle it, it'll piss on itself. Let me try."

Pick your nose and wipe it on the dog's head.

At some point, your victim will display some sort of affection toward his pet. When he does, say, "You know, those people in San Francisco with the dogs that killed the lacrosse coach were supposed to have had sex with those dogs." Then cast a very suspicious look at your victim.

Suggest, "I think your dog is gay. Scientists say that some animals are. I think Rex is one of those." When your victim asks how you can tell that his dog is gay, reply, "Oh, just the way he walks, the way he barks. I have pretty good gay-dar."

Tell your victim about the time you ran over a dog with your car: "It looked just like yours, too. I felt sort of bad at first, but then I thought about it, and I realized it was only a dog." When your victim asks you if you stopped to help it, reply, "No, it was obviously a goner."

Comment, "I read recently that most dogs actually hate their owners, but have to be nice to them because that's who gives them food. But one thing's for sure, if your dog was your size, he'd kill you and eat you." Your victim may argue. Inform him, "There was a dog owner in Hartford who was found about a week after he had died; during that time, his dogs had eaten most of him … Yep, dogs really are loyal."

The Hunter

If your victim is a hunter, and his den is decorated with mounted deer heads and the like, he has probably taken grief about his hobby from other people. Add your voice to the chorus.

Gesture at one of his trophies and comment, "It was either you or him, huh?"

Then ask, "What'd you take him with, a bow or rifle?" (Chances are he used a rifle; this will remind him that bow hunters look down on riflemen.)

After he answers, just nod judiciously and comment, "I figure a tough guy like you, you might have just scared him to death."

"What was he armed with? Nothing? That doesn't seem very sporting."

"Did it make you feel manly when you killed him?"

"They say people who hunt animals in their heart of hearts really want to kill humans."

"Ah well, I'm sure they'd have felt honored if they'd known who they were going to be taken by."

"Would you want to spend eternity mounted on the wall of the guy who killed you?"

Point at one and ask, "Did you eat his meat? Or just kill him for sport?" If he ate it, ignore his answer; if he didn't, comment, "I was afraid of that."

Muse, "He has such a gentle look in his eyes. I wonder if his mother misses him. Didn't you ever see *Bambi* when you were a kid?"

"What did he ever do to you? Seriously, did he do something to provoke you? Did he tease you about [your victim's Achilles Heel]?"

"Look directly at the deer with an affronted look and say, "How dare you say that to me? You have besmirched my honor, sir. I challenge you to a duel!" Turn your back to the deer, walk ten paces holding up an imaginary pistol, then whirl around and pretend to shoot.

Then ask, "Or was it more Wyatt Earp at the OK Corral?" Stand facing the deer from across the room, your legs spread wide, your hands held to your sides as if waiting to draw your six shooters. Pantomime drawing some imaginary six shooters, blaze away, blow the smoke from the tips of your guns, then twirl them and put them back in their holsters.

Or do your imitation of De Niro in *Taxi Driver*. Look at the deer and say, "You talkin' to me? You talkin' to me? I don't see nobody else around here. You talkin' to me?" Then extend an imaginary pistol from your sleeve and blast away.

If at any time during this performance you feel your victim is about to snap, back off. You don't want to end up as one of his trophies.

The Cliché User

Anybody who speaks in clichés is a tiresome creature. If your victim is one of these, point this out.

If your victim says, "There are many fish in the sea," reply, "Ah, what a wise proverb."

Or, "Thought of that all by yourself, did you?"

Or clap and say, "Bravo. I applaud your originality."

Or, "Why do you respond to every situation with a cliché? Can't you think for yourself?"

"Hmm, never heard that one before."

If he keeps it up, ask, "Have you ever said anything original in your entire life?"

Most clichés are half-truths. So point out the half that isn't really true. Hold the cliché up to the cold light of day, analyze it, and pick it apart. For instance, if he says, "That which doesn't kill me makes me stronger," respond, "How exactly does that work? Obviously, nothing has killed you yet; but you seem kinda weak. Especially in the brain if you use clichés like that."

Or shrug and say, "Well, that which hasn't killed you seems to have increased your use of clichés."

If you point out your victim's hypocrisy and he responds that consistency is the hobgoblin of small minds, reply, "Clichés like that are the hobgoblin of people who can't think for themselves."

If your victim says, "There's no I in T-E-A-M," reply, "But there is an M-E."

If he says, "Women—can't live with 'em, can't live without 'em," shrug, "I've lived without them for most of my life."

Or ask, "Is that your personal mantra? Hmm, that's funny—it's everyone else's mantra too."

Or respond, "That is one tired cliché. I mean, that thing is just bone weary."

Or, "So this is where all the clichés come to rest."

If you can't drive your victim away with these retorts, you can at least keep him from reciting too many clichés. And if he can't use clichés, he probably won't have much to say, which is almost as good as driving him away.

Mr. Repetitious

The fellow who tells the same stories or jokes over and over again is the definition of tedious. You can curb his repetitious tendencies by pointing them out.

One way is to interrupt him towards the end of his story, saying, "I know, I know, I've heard this before."

Or hit your forehead with the butt of your hand, as if trying to drive the pain of hearing him talk out of your head.

But it is probably better to employ a lighter touch:

"The more you tell that story, the better it gets. I swear, I know it by heart myself now."

"I'm getting that déjà vu feeling."

"Please don't forget to tell me that story yet again tomorrow."

"You must think I'm incredibly stupid that I don't get the message the first four times you tell me."

"This is becoming my favorite bedtime story. It puts me to sleep every time."

"It's too bad they don't make records anymore, because to say that someone sounds like a 'broken CD' just doesn't have the same ring."

"Take thirty-five, coming up."

"I feel like I'm in that movie *Groundhog Day*."

Ask him, "Do you think that repeating something will make it so? They say that if you tell a lie enough times, it becomes a truth."

The Plagiarist

When one writer steals another's writing, it's called plagiarism and is legally actionable. When your victim uses other people's lines, expecting you to think him witty, it's called, well, nothing. That doesn't mean you can't call him on it.

If your victim imitates someone you both know, say, "Aha, I see you're flattering Bill in the most sincere way. He'll be happy to hear it."

If he tries it again, say, in your most tired voice, "I was *there*, Joey. I was *there* when Bill said that."

If your victim is getting his material from a popular movie, just cite the film and the scene: "Oh yeah, that's from *Training Day*, the scene where Denzel Washington first meets Ethan Hawke in the diner."

If your victim cribs a joke from a written source, just tell him, "I read that article too."

If he continues to borrow, ask, "Are you going to write a bibliography, credit all your various sources for your material?"

If your victim delivers a funny line, one you are fairly sure could not have originated with him, but you don't know the source, ask, "Where'd you hear that one? I never know with you—one day you're Arnold Schwarzenegger in *The Last Action Hero*, the next you're Kurt Russell in *Three Thousand Miles to Graceland*. Who are you today?"

"You don't really know who you are, do you? You take little bits and pieces of other people's personalities and try to cobble them together as your own, but what you end up with is a patchwork that doesn't quite fit together."

Should He Express an Unoriginal Opinion

If your victim regurgitates someone else's opinion on a subject, reply, "Well, that's the conventional wisdom." When he then asks you what you think, reply, "The smart money thinks [the opposite]," implying that he is "dumb" money.

Or you can reply, "That's what's they're trying to brainwash people into thinking these days," implying that he is not much better than a robot.

There are many ways to express this sentiment:

"That's not what the intelligentsia think." (Use of the word 'intelligentsia' is always extremely presumptuous, for it inevitably implies that the speaker himself is a member.)

"That's most people's knee-jerk response."

"That's the herd mentality."

"That seems to be the direction the lemmings are headed."

"Ah, quoting the party line I see."

"That's certainly the politically correct way to view things."

"That's the 'safe and respectable' thing to think."

"Don't tell me you've jumped on the bandwagon too."

Use of any of these lines is guaranteed to make your victim defensive, and he'll probably respond with another cliché. Reply, "Let me get this straight. I accuse you of unoriginal thinking, so you defend yourself by using a cliché?"

Democrats

Whichever side of the aisle your victim is on, you can annoy him by associating him with the most extreme wing of his party.

If your victim is a Democrat, start by asking him, "Are you more of a Cuba-style Democrat or a North Korea-style Democrat?"

Ask, "Do you go to a lot of demonstrations and hold placards and chant and stuff? Ever take part in a really good riot?"

"Comrade, are you more of a Leninist or a Stalinist? It always amazes me, the number one lesson of the twentieth century was that socialism doesn't work, but the Democrats just refuse to accept that."

"Why is it that every Democratic president of the past fifty years, with the sole exception of Jimmy Carter, was an inveterate liar or womanizer, sometimes both? What does that say about the Democratic Party?"

Ask, "Why do you like higher taxes?"

"Why do Democrats insist that women are as qualified as men to become firemen and physically carry people out of burning buildings?"

"Have you ever heard the saying that anybody who isn't liberal as a youngster doesn't have a heart, and anybody who doesn't become conservative as a grownup doesn't have a brain? So … how old are *you*?"

One of the great icons of the Democratic Party is John F. Kennedy. So point out, "You know, by today's standards, JFK was really right wing. He was for equal rights without favoritism, he was an ardent Cold Warrior, he started the Vietnam War, and he wasn't exactly a feminist in his personal life."

Or simply agree with your victim. Say, "Yeah, I'm a Democrat, too. I believe in political correctness: free the people on Death Row so they can become tree huggers like the rest of us. I've always felt that people are too stupid to know what to do with themselves; the government should tell us what to do."

Republicans

If your victim is a Republican, simply subscribe to the same sorts of grotesque oversimplifications.

Say, "Oh, you're a Republican? So I guess you're one of those guys who likes to lounge around at his country club sipping martinis and complaining about how everybody else doesn't work hard enough."

"Are you a member of the KKK as well? I get the impression all Republicans in their heart of hearts really want a return to segregation and the Jim Crow laws."

"Don't most Republicans think that Hitler was basically right, but just went a little too far?"

Associate your victim with the religious right: "So if your daughter got raped, you'd force her to have the baby of her rapist? Republicans are always spouting off about family values—is that the kind of family you want?"

"So you think AIDS is a scourge sent by God?"

"I'm a Democrat; I believe in separation of church and state."

"Republicans always go on about law and order, but in the meantime, who's committing the biggest crimes of all, the thieves who take fifty dollars? No, it's the corporate criminals who rip off their shareholders for billions of dollars. Yet they usually get the lightest sentences. I think the punishment ought to be commensurate with the amount of money stolen."

"The thing that kills me about you Republicans is how you believe in creationism rather than evolution. Sorry, but evolution is a fact. Like it or not, you're descended from monkeys. Everybody with an IQ in the triple digits has pretty much believed it since Darwin took that trip to the Galapagos in the 1850's. Tell me—do you also believe the world is flat?"

"The Republicans all seem to believe that the U.S. has the right to boss everybody around just because we're bigger and stronger. Hell, if you guys had your way, we'd probably conquer Canada."

Whenever you refer to fellow Democrats, work in the adjectives "progressive" and "enlightened."

Or be agreeable: "I'm a Republican, too. I think a woman's place is in the kitchen, barefoot and pregnant."

Conclude, "The reason Republicans don't like Democrats is because they can't believe anybody else would be nice enough to want to help people."

The Religious Zealot

Most people have some religious background, but don't qualify as zealots. The person whose life revolves around his religion is almost always in dire need of mockery. Of course, making fun of someone's religious beliefs is easy; the difficult part is dealing with them afterwards.

All religions are vulnerable. But since most people in this country are Christians, this chapter will focus on suggested comments to them. Maintain a straight face and ask the following questions "innocently," as if merely intellectually curious.

"What I've never understood about hell is, how can you burn forever? I mean, if you get in a fire, you just turn into ashes, and that's that. You can't burn twice."

"Do you really think your pastor talks to God? What do you think they talk about? Sports? Politics? The weather? Maybe they gossip. If God sees everything, I bet he's got some really good gossip."

"When you pray, do you really think that God hears you?"

"Do you really believe that Christ's mother was a virgin? You think she ever did any heavy petting? Cause technically, you can do that and still maintain your virginity."

"When Christ walked on water, how long did he do it for? And how deep was it? Just in case he fell in, did he know how to swim?"

"And after he died, before he was resurrected, did he go through rigor mortis? If he did, he must have been awfully sore when he woke up."

"Why do all those boxers believe that the Lord is on their side? Do they really believe that God cares about the outcome of a prizefight? If I were the Lord, I'd be so insulted that some boxer thought I'd bother to fix a fight that I'd actually make him lose. And now that I think about it, isn't having the Lord on your side an unfair advantage? It doesn't really seem very sporting."

"Do you feel that your God is better than, say, Allah?"

When your victim tells you what particular branch of Christianity he belongs to, no matter which sect it is, say, "Oh yeah, I see you guys on television on Sunday mornings sometimes. You're the ones who cry out 'Amen!' and 'Praise the Lord!' and start dancing in the aisles whenever the spirit moves you, even in the middle of the minister's sermons."

"I saw a show about you guys once, where you were handling the rattlesnakes and chanting and stuff."

Or, "Aren't you the ones who lash yourselves and call it scourging or something? And don't some of you reenact the crucifixion of Christ by actually driving nails through the palms of your hands?"

Or, "You're the guys who go around laying hands on crippled people and helping them to walk again, and getting blind people to see and stuff. I saw a movie about you guys once—*Elmer Gantry*"

If your victim is a Mormon, ask him, "How many wives do you plan on having?" (If your victim is a woman, ask, "Do you plan to be somebody's sixth wife?")

Ask, "Do you tithe to the church? Why not?"

If your victim is Catholic, ask, "So, how many times were *you* molested?"

Add, "What church did you go to, Our Lady of the Cute Altar Boys?"

Ask, "What is that branch of Catholicism where they combine it with voodoo and sacrifice goats and pigs and stuff? Santeria? Do you ever practice that?" When your victim expresses his opinion of Santeria, reply, "Well, that's pretty much how I feel about all religion."

Ask, "You believe that Christ performed miracles, right? Well I think it'll be a miracle if you ever develop any common sense and realize that your religion is just a primitive superstition."

Do keep in mind, Christians are about the only people it's safe to make fun of these days. Many believers in other religions take themselves so seriously that you're risking your well-being by making fun of them.

"So You Belong to a Cult"

Should your victim ever mention any group or organization with which he is affiliated, however loosely, the proper response is, "Oh, I didn't know you belonged to a cult."

If he mentions something interesting he heard on Dr. Laura (or Rush Limbaugh or Howard Stern), reply, "I read somewhere recently that her followers have a lot in common with the people who followed Jim Jones down in Guyana."

When he denies this, reply, "Well, just don't drink the Kool-Aid."

Say, "You must have a big emptiness in your life to want to fill it by listening to someone like her." (This is one of those intangible claims it is impossible to deny.)

If your victim has been reading a self-help book and mentions the author, say, "Oh yeah, I've heard of him. He's a Scientologist." When your victim denies this and insists he's a reputable doctor, ask what the doctor recommends in the book. Then nod your head knowingly and reply, "Yep, they preach a lot of that same stuff in Scientology." Add, "L. Ron Hubbard may have been an inventive science fiction writer, but I sure wouldn't base my life around his teachings."

When your victim protests that this is not the case, ignore him and muse, "If I were going to pick a sci-fi guy, I'd go with Robert Heinlein."

Should your victim be a member of ROTC (or the National Guard or the Army Reserve or any of the armed forces), offer, "They say that people who join ROTC are particularly susceptible to being brainwashed. Seriously, I read recently that they use a lot of the same basic techniques there that the Soviets used on their conscripts." Ask, "Do they hypnotize you?" Stand up like a movie zombie, your arms in front of you, slowly walk forward, and chant, "Kill, kill …" in a mindless monotone. Then make a circular motion with your finger near your temple, and say knowingly, "It's the same mentality."

If your victim is a Trekkie or Deadhead, say, "You know, there *are* agencies that can help you get away from those cults. I'm not just talking about the ones that kidnap you and return you to your parents."

PART VI
The Ham-Handed Compliment/Insult

The Meaningless Compliment

How many times have you been irked by some well-intentioned but boneheaded fellow who gives you a "compliment" that is utterly without value? You, too, can shower your victim with such "praise."

One way to do this is to compliment your victim for his association with something or somebody he deserves no credit for. Introduce your victim to a third party by saying, "Victim's brother is a partner at one of the largest law firms in Ohio," as if any of the credit should redound to him.

One of the best ways to render a compliment meaningless is to make it a group compliment. If your victim clearly deserves to be singled out for his contribution to a team effort, tell him, "You guys did a great job. A really great job," as if he contributed no more than his teammates. If he is clearly the best in the group, tell him, "You're among the best in this group."

In a situation where your victim is a team member whose contribution is subpar, you can highlight this fact by seeming to struggle for a reason to give him praise. After effusively lavishing praise on the team leader, look at your victim and say, "And you did a good job of … holding down the fort." (Or "providing team spirit" or "being there for backup.")

Praise your victim for some universal rite of passage that is not really merit worthy. Graduations are one such. Upon seeing him in his cap and gown, tell him, "Congratulations! You did it—you really did it!" (Graduation needn't be from high school or college, it can be from a continuing ed course.)

Congratulate your victim on his purchase of a new car. This is the kind of thing that people often congratulate each other for, but really, what has one accomplished other than wasting a bunch of money?

Congratulate him on getting married. If you lay the congratulations on thick enough, the implication left hanging in the air is that you are surprised he was able to land a spouse. ("Wow, congratulations, you actually did it!") Adding the word "actually" to any compliment implies that it is a millennial event.

Rave about some other person, and give a lot of specifics as to why he is the most accomplished guy you know. With that as backdrop, say that your victim is a "nice guy."

Damning with faint praise is an art that has been used for eons by practitioners of the meaningless compliment.

Qualify the Compliment

You can turn a compliment into an insult merely by qualifying it. There are all sorts of compliments that can be tailored to your victim (i.e., "You're very smart for a model," or, "You're very well-mannered for an Italian.")

But there are also all sorts of generic qualifications that can be applied to just about any situation and leave your victim fuming. Let's say you and he are part of a golf foursome. When he first tees off, say, "That's a really nice shot, for a beginner."

Or, "That's really good, for you."

Or just say, "Good job," in a tone that indicates utter amazement.

Put your arm around him, then say, "You did a really good job. I was proud of you." The body language here is extremely condescending. The one caveat here is that you must be physically larger than your victim; otherwise it is hard to pull off.

After your victim pars a few holes, give him that traditional left-handed compliment, "Well, you get the Most Improved Award." (The implication, of course, is that he stunk before.)

When he continues to demonstrate his excellence, offer, in measured tones, "Keep working at it. Some day you could really be good."

If your victim does something really spectacular, like hit a hole in one, offer, "That's not bad."

Toward the end of the game, say, "You're better than I thought."

Then say, "People are wrong about you." He'll then ask you what people say; reply cryptically, "Oh, you know what the grapevine is like."

After the game is over, after he has shot three under par, say, "Well, you get an A for effort."

The worst part about all this for your victim is that after each compliment/insult, he is supposed to thank you.

Over-Praise Him

You can embarrass your victim by overstating his accomplishments to another person. If your victim was an accomplished swimmer, say, "John here was an Olympic swimmer." This puts your victim in an awkward position. He must either correct you or go along with the lie. If he corrects you, look at him blankly and say, "Oh. Somehow I'd gotten that impression from you," leaving your victim feeling that he is both a fraud and a disappointment.

If your victim doesn't correct you, even better. After a few seconds elapse, during which the other person has probably expressed admiration for this feat, say, "You *were* an Olympic swimmer, weren't you?" At this point, he either has to come clean, in which case he is tacitly admitting that he was abetting a self-serving falsehood earlier, or you've really got him. If he says yes, ask him which year's Olympic team he was on. Then ask who the most famous swimmer was on that team. Then say, "Oh yeah, what was he like?" The more he compounds his lie, the harder it will be for him to back out. (In fact, at this point, it's already pretty much impossible.) When he's eventually caught, it will be brutal.

If your victim is a Vietnam veteran, say, "John here won the Medal of Honor in Vietnam."

If he's an accompanist with the Boston Symphony Orchestra, say, "John soloed with the Boston Symphony."

If your victim graduated from Brown cum laude, say he graduated from Harvard summa cum laude.

If your victim has done a little runway work, say, "Susie is a supermodel." If she's appeared in a few television shows, say, "Susie is a movie star."

A related tactic is, when your victim has turned in a subpar performance, to congratulate him on a great performance. If he usually runs the mile in four minutes and fifteen seconds, but is sick and can only go four minutes and twenty-eight seconds, rush up to him afterwards and tell him you never saw him look so good. This will put him in the awkward position of having to either thank you and imply that a four twenty-eight actually is good, or launch into a lengthy explanation of how it isn't.

Your victim will probably not fully realize what you're doing to him.

Under-Praise Him

Under-praising your victim can be just as annoying. Let's say your victim ran a quarter mile in forty-nine seconds. Tell a third party, "John here ran a quarter mile in fifty seconds." Your victim must either suffer in silence, frustrated he's being shortchanged, or look egotistical by correcting you. It's not a happy choice.

If he soloed with the Boston Symphony Orchestra, say, "John is an accompanist with the Boston Symphony." And so on.

Again, he can hardly get angry, because you are ostensibly praising him.

A related tactic is to mention an effort without mentioning the resulting lack of success, once again setting up failure. Say, "Jim here once applied for a Rhodes Scholarship." The third party will then naturally ask what happened, and Jim will be forced to say that he was turned down. At this point, you should magnanimously interject, "Hey, anybody who even applies for a Rhodes Scholarship is a winner in my book."

Or boast about your victim's qualifications as a Lothario: "Joe here once tried to date a Miss America." When the third party asks what happened, Joe must admit to, and possibly make excuses for, having been rejected. (Excuses always make someone sound a little pathetic.)

Or say, "John here is trying to be a writer." The third party will inevitably ask if he's had any success, and your victim will look foolish as he tries to explain why he hasn't.

If your victim is nice-looking, when you introduce him, add, "As you can see, he is incredibly handsome." If he's anything shy of Jude Law, he will come up short, and chances are he's not quick-witted enough to say something like "You mock me," so he'll just have to stand there and look foolish—as well as not all that good-look-ing—instead.

"I Know"

These two simple words can be the most obnoxious in the English language, if spoken after your victim makes a modest comment. They should be uttered quietly and without emphasis. As angry as your victim will be, there's really not much he can say in response, since all you've done is agree with him. So he must just fume silently.

If your victim is berating himself for his lack of nerve, and cries out, "I'm such a wimp," quietly respond, "I know."

Your victim may fumble something and say, "I'm such a klutz!"

Your victim may make a mistake and say, "I swear, I'm retarded!"

He may make a faux pas, and castigate himself by saying, "I'm such a social moron!"

He may look in the mirror and say, "I'm so fat!"

You know what to say.

You needn't wait for your victim to say something self-deprecating. Prompt him. Compliment him on how well he did on a test. Then, when he replies, "I'm not really very smart, I just study hard," say, "I know." (Know-it-alls are never more annoying than when they know your weaknesses.)

Thank him for some favor he did you. When he says, "It was nothing," utter the magic words.

If He Gets Injured

People usually feel that sympathy is attention they have "earned" from whatever injury they have sustained. Men in particular like to see themselves in a heroic light. The typical male wants you to fret and cluck over his bloody cut, while he shrugs it off and says, "It's only a flesh wound," so you can marvel at his toughness and stoicism. (Is there any doubt most of us have watched too many movies?) If you yourself tell him it's only a flesh wound, you deprive him of his moment of glory.

So do exactly that. If your victim sustains a bad cut, shrug it off for him. Nonchalantly say, "Don't worry, it's not very deep. You'll survive."

"That's what you're all upset about? Jesus, from the way you were squawking, I thought it was something serious."

Or take his injury as your cue to talk about your own past injuries, besides which his pale.

The opposite approach can also disturb. If your victim's skin has been broken, announce gravely, "That's the kind of cut that always leaves an ugly scar."

"You better be careful. That kind of cut can turn gangrenous very quickly."

Add, for effect, "You'd have a hard time playing football [or whatever sport he likes to do] with only one arm."

If your victim exhibits a purplish bruise and boasts about how hard a hit he withstood to merit this particular badge of honor, peer closely and inform him, "That's not a bruise. That's Kaposi's Sarcoma." (This is an AIDS-related discoloration.)

If the bruise is near a joint, suggest, "That could be a sign of lymph cancer. You really should go to a hospital and get it checked out." (This tactic works best if he is on vacation in a third world country.) If he does make the effort to go to a doctor, and it turns out to be nothing, he can't be overtly resentful since you theoretically have his best interests in mind.

Or peer at his bump closely and observe, "That's the kind of bruising that occurs mostly with females. It gets raised like that because of all the estrogen."

If your victim complains of tiredness, ask, "Do you ever feel too tired to get out of bed in the morning?" (We all do.) "Do you ever have unexplained aches and pains?" (We all do.) "Have you spent any time outside in the past few months?" (We all have.) Conclude, "You probably have Lyme disease. You should get tested." Once you have planted this seed in his mind, every time he gets tired it will occur to him that he might have Lyme, and it will gnaw at him until he finally does get himself checked out.

If you want to declare war, ask, rhetorically, "You're screaming about that?" Shake your head in disbelief and say, slowly and emphatically, "You have got to be the world's biggest pussy."

Castration Made Simple

If your victim ever acts less than macho, imply he is something less than a man. Start by feminizing his name (turn John into Joan, Michael into Michelle, etc.). Then refer to him sarcastically as "old brass balls over here" or "mosquito balls."

"I thought they only spayed dogs."

"Why don't you grow a pair of balls?"

"You'd probably be more comfortable wearing a dress and pair of high heels."

Ask, "On Sundays, do you and your friends all get together for brunch and sing show tunes?"

The most effective way to castrate your victim is simply to act very gallant towards him, as an old-fashioned gent might act to a lady. Act normally with other guy in the room. But treat your victim like a lady. Open his car door for him, light his cigarettes, hold out his chair as he is about to sit down, offer to open a jar for him. Ask him if he's too hot or cold; if he's too cold, offer him your jacket. Be solicitous to him in such a way that others can see. Don't say these things mockingly, say them politely, as if you're genuinely concerned for his welfare. (They'll have more bite this way.)

Don't act as if he's a woman you're trying to seduce, but rather as if you're just trying to be nice to your grandmother. Your victim will not be able to get angry at you because, after all, you're only trying to be nice. But he will be left feeling disconcertingly wimpy.

If He Shows You His Photographs

Who among us has not met the egotist who thinks we actually want to look at photographs of his kids? If your victim asks if you'd like to see his, offer the response he deserves: "No thanks."

When he looks crestfallen, relent brusquely: "Okay, go ahead, show me your pictures if you have to."

At this point, your victim will probably say, "Forget it," in which case you're off the hook. If he actually hands you the pictures, at least you've established the proper mood.

Your victim expects you to gushingly confirm his opinion that he has the cutest children on earth. (Most people feel they have no choice but to lavish such compliments.)

In fact, you do have a choice.

Take the photos, look at them stonily, then hand them back without a word. If you feel you absolutely must make some sort of response, just nod curtly.

If the children actually are cute, ask, "Oh … were they adopted?" When your victim says no and wonders why you ask, answer, "They don't look like you."

If any are slightly overweight, ask, "Does this one have Down syndrome?" When your victim responds huffily that he doesn't, take the moral high road: "Are you saying that it's wrong to have Down syndrome? Are you saying those children don't deserve to be loved too? They can't help it, you know."

If your victim shows you photos of his children, he's probably equally uninhibited about showing you his vacation pictures.

Start by asking, "Were these pictures taken with an Instamatic? You should get one of those auto-focus cameras ... Oh, it is?"

Say, "It's tough when they catch you mid-blink. It makes you look as if you're drunk or something ... *Were* you drunk there?"

"What's that funny expression you always put on your face when you have your picture taken?"

Ask sympathetically, "Was the photographer one of those idiots who always says, 'Say cheese,' and then makes you hold the smile for about ten seconds before he snaps the shutter? I always find my smiles turning into grimaces too."

"It's hard to look good when you're front lit."

If a photograph makes him look undeniably bad, say, with a straight face, "Hey, you look pretty good in that one."

If your victim is sensitive about his weight, look at the picture as if you're seeing him for the first time, and say, "Hey—you need to lose some weight!"

If the picture shows him in a bathing suit, wince and say, "You really shouldn't let them take a picture of you like that. Don't you have any caftans or anything?"

It's always best to say these things with others present. Laughingly compare your victim to a well-known cartoon character as you pass the picture along to the others: "Hey look—the Pillsbury Doughboy!" Other favorable comparisons include Mr. Magoo, the Michelin Tire Man, Barney Rubble, and the Wicked Witch.

If it's a highly flattering picture, just ask, "Is that you?" When he says yes, reply, "Are you sure?"

Foreigners

Being an ugly American is both easy and fun, especially with the snobby European pseudo sophisticates who look down on American culture.

If your victim is from a formerly communist country, ask, "Do they still practice communism over there? Do you guys still see Stalin as a hero?"

Add, "I hear the air pollution there is so bad, it's like smoking a pack of cigarettes a day. I guess that's why everybody in Slovakia smokes anyway. Have they discovered over there that smoking causes cancer yet?"

"I've heard that anybody who wants decent medical treatment in your country comes over here."

If he's from a country where English is spoken, ask, "Your TV mostly just shows American reruns, right?"

If your victim is from England, France, Spain, Germany, or Portugal, and he's conservative, point out, "You guys really had a glorious colonial history. But look at you now, your country is just a weak, impotent has-been."

If he's a leftist, take the opposite tack: "You people had the bloodiest, most brutal colonial history of anyone."

If your victim is from any European country except Germany or Italy, say, "We really saved your butts in World War II. If it hadn't been for us, you'd all be going around speaking German and saying *Heil* Hitler right now."

If he's from Germany or Italy, ask, "Did you really think you could take on the United States in a war? I just can't imagine what was going through your heads."

If your victim feels obliged to talk up his country's good points, concede, "You know, you do have a point. Maybe we should just conquer you guys and make you our fifty-first state."

At some point, your victim may talk about the superiority of his native cuisine. Shake your head dismissively: "I don't really consider that stuff food." If he insists you try some, say, "I did once. I was sick for three days afterward."

Wherever he's from, comment, "I hear they have the greatest whorehouses over there—really cheap, too. In fact, I've heard all the good-looking women in your country become prostitutes."

Another good line to use, especially if he is rich, is, "So tell me Jean-Louis, why did you come over to our country? To take advantage of our welfare system?"

Foreigners from a Third World Country

It's always amusing to confuse the culture of a less developed country with a Stone Age one. Almost any visitor from a third world country will in fact be from the upper classes, which means he is richer—and likely more sophisticated—than you. Ignore this inconvenient fact.

For instance, if your victim is from India, ask, "Do people really live in trees back where you come from?" Or, "Do you really eat grubs?"

Casually comment, "I understand they still practice cannibalism back there." Ask, "Who tastes better, men or women?"

"The first time you saw a car, did you think it was an angry animal?"

"When there's thunder and lightning, do you think the gods are angry?"

"Was your tribe very warlike?"

If you're near a computer, show it to him as if he's never seen one before. Ask, "Do you have telephones back in your country?"

Ask, "Do you have a king or do you have one of those presidents-for-life?" When your victim informs you that they have elections, reply, "But they're totally rigged!"

"If you want to go to your friend's place, do you just hop on an elephant and go?"

"I can't believe your little country gets as many votes in the U.N. as the U.S." To really put his country in perspective, ask, "When did we discover you?"

"Don't like 25 percent of the people there have AIDS?"

The easiest victim is the one from Latin America.

No matter how many times your victim tells you that he's from Honduras, or Nicaragua, keep referring to his country as "Mexico."

If you see your victim writing, act impressed: "Wow, you must be someone special in Mexico. Do people ask you to write letters for them? You must be the town scribe."

If he ever says anything positive about his country, present the following irrefutable argument: "If your country's so great, what are you doing up here?"

Your victim may take a combative tone after your comments; reply, "We give your country tons of foreign aid, and you're just a bunch of ingrates. We should just cut it all off, let you starve."

If you feel this is too harsh, backtrack by showing some humanitarian concern: "Weren't you worried about drowning when you crossed the Rio Grande?"

If English Is His Second Language

People who speak with foreign accents are often very self-conscious about it. It is your job to make them more so.

Say your victim is French. When he apologizes for his strong accent, accept his apology thusly: "It's okay, but most of the time I can't tell whether you're speaking French or English." Occasionally ask, as if extremely frustrated by his accent, "Would you speak English for Crissakes?!"

Say, "You really should hire an interpreter to follow you around."

Imitate your victim's accent.

Speak slowly and exaggeratedly to your victim, as if talking to a particularly backward four-year-old. Ask, "Do you know what time it is?" When he tells you the time, shake your head in frustration, and say, "No—you don't understand—what I'm asking is, *do—you—know—what—time—it—is*?" He will be confused by your reaction and will say something like, what? At this point, shake your head in disgust, and say, "Never mind," as if it's not even worth trying to communicate with him.

Use rudimentary sign language as you speak to your victim, as if that is the only way he could understand you. Say, "It's raining," and point at the sky, then make a motion indicating that water is falling down, then point at the dark spots on your shirt.

Speak pidgin: "You likee eatie? Me go restaurant." Helpfully add, "Eat," shoveling imaginary food into your mouth.

If English Is His
First Language

It will sting even more if you treat a fellow American as if English were his second language.

If you have occasion to use big words, immediately substitute a one-syllable word: "Well Sam, that was very perspicacious of you … you know, smart. Sorry, I normally do a better job of relating to people."

After saying that you would "look askance" at something, helpfully add, "I'm saying I would disapprove of it."

Talk about your victim's field of expertise as if he is a novice. If he is a stockbroker, refer to "shorting," then explain that this means selling a share of stock you do not own in hopes of buying it back cheaper later on. Or refer to calls or puts, then explain to him that these are options to buy or sell a stock at a certain price.

Translate common usage foreign phrases for him. Say, *"C'est la vie,"* then add helpfully, "That means 'that's life.'" Further add, as if even that concept might be above him, "You know, shit happens."

The effect is magnified if you're in public; translate everything for your victim, and him alone, as if only he is too dense to understand what the others are saying. If somebody refers to "esprit de corps," explain, in an audible aside to your victim, "That means team spirit."

At a restaurant, helpfully explain to your victim that the "soup du jour" is the soup of the day. Explain that "a la carte" means you are ordering the dish by itself, and that "filet mignon" is a kind of steak. In a Japanese restaurant, explain that "sushi" is raw fish, as if your victim is a rube who has never been anywhere but McDonald's.

At some point, he will undoubtedly explode, "I know that! You don't have to keep explaining what these phrases mean to me!" Mildly reply, "Sorry, I was only trying to be helpful." Then shake your head as if he is being completely unreasonable.

Condescend

Never compliment your victim on anything you're not clearly better at. Don't praise his tennis game until you have demonstrated that you are the superior player. Don't compliment him on his Harvard law degree unless he knows you were a Rhodes Scholar. Don't compliment him on his new Mercedes until you pull up in a Rolls. (Once you have established your superiority, the more lavish your praise, the more condescending it will come across.)

If your victim knows you're an ace skier, and you find out that he has just learned how to snowplow, respond, "That's great! That's really good!" You want to leave him feeling like a child being congratulated by his parent for finally having his training wheels taken off. If you can establish a parent/child relationship, the odor of patronization will hang heavy in the air.

If he puts himself down, climb on board: "Well, everybody has to start somewhere." Never forget that you are the mentor and he is but the novice, or even better, novitiate. Should he ever lose sight of his status, remind him with a gentle, "You've really come a long way—you should be proud of yourself." (None of us should ever forget where we came from.)

If your victim offers to pick up the check, don't offer to pay yourself. Just ask, with a tone of great concern, "Are you sure you can afford it?"

Two Kinds of People

Whenever anybody starts out by saying that there are two kinds of people in this world, he is basically saying that there is a successful type and an unsuccessful type, and that he is the former and you are the latter.

The proof of the basic obnoxiousness of this statement is how often the bad guys in the movies make it. (Usually the bad guy uses this line as justification for being a predator, i.e., having no morals.) Think of Denzel Washington as the sociopathic detective in *Training Day* telling his innocent partner that he can be either a sheep or a wolf.

You can trot this line out on all sorts of occasions. If your victim happens to need a flashlight, tell him, as you hand one to him with a flourish, "There are two kinds of people in this world, my friend, those who are prepared and those who aren't." (The grating "my friend" will annoy him even further.)

If he needs matches and you happen to have some, you know what to say. Or if he needs an umbrella. Or the correct change. Or anything at all.

A variation on the "two kinds of people" theme is, "This is what separates the men from the boys." This, of course, is always a reference to the speaker's manhood and the listener's lack thereof. This comment can be used any time you outperform your victim, be it at weight lifting or tiddlywinks.

There are two kinds of people in the world: those who separate it into two kinds of people, and those who don't. When you're with your victim, make sure you're the former.

Jocks

Athletes (or ex-athletes) inevitably have a soft spot in their hearts for their sports, which they identify pretty closely with. They also tend to have fairly macho sensibilities. This combination makes them quite vulnerable to various "unintentional" putdowns.

Confuse your victim's sport with another. Confuse lacrosse with field hockey, swimming with diving, polo with water polo, hockey with figure skating, and the decathlon, biathlon, heptathlon, pentathlon, and triathlon with each other. If he's British and he played cricket, confuse that with croquet.

If your victim played lacrosse, say, "I thought that was just a girls' sport."

If he was a gymnast, ask if it's "rhythmic or the regular kind." When he explains that rhythmic is just for women, reply, "Oh, so you just do the uneven parallel bars and stuff like that."

If your victim wrestled, opine, "Personally, I think The Rock is the greatest wrestler of all time."

If your victim played football, observe, "The football players were always the dumbest guys at my college." (This comment can also be applied to basketball, hockey, and baseball players.)

Ask your victim if his was a Division I team; if not, comment, "Now Division I football, that's *real* football." If he played Division I, make the comment about SEC football.

Football players like to think themselves tough, so tell your victim the following anecdote: "At my high school, there was this guy who wrestled at a hundred and fifty-four pounds, and the football players called him a sissy because of the little singlet he had to wear. So during the course of the year, this guy got every single football player alone at some point, and then just beat the living crap out of him. It was great!"

If your victim played rugby, comment, "The guys who played rugby at my college were just guys who couldn't make the football team."

If your victim plays hockey, or tennis, or swims, or fences, or does gymnastics, just say, "You're lucky not too many black people do that. If they did, they'd dominate it the way they do basketball, boxing, and track. You'd just be second string."

If your victim did anything besides football or basketball, say, "Those guys were low men on the totem pole at my school. I don't think anybody ever went to watch them play except their parents."

If your victim swam or ran track, ask what his time was in his event. Then ask, "Aren't the girls doing that now?" (If he wasn't that fast, make it "twelve-year-old girls.")

If your victim was a cheerleader, just laugh as if you assume he's joking. When he says he's serious, turn your laugh into a smirk. No comment necessary.

If he did cross-country, just look at him appraisingly and say, "Yeah, you're built like a cross-country guy. Or a jockey, I guess."

If he did a sport that is generally considered to result in an ideal build, such as swimming, look at him and say, "But you don't really have a swimmer's build." If he's put on a few pounds, give him the once over and ask, "What was your, uh, fighting weight?"

If he's on the small side, and did any sport other than cross-country or wrestling, ask, sympathetically, "Don't you have to be big and strong to do that?"

If your victim is a successful female athlete, point out, "The women who do best at sports are the ones who are built the most like guys." Should she object to this characterization, just give her some famous examples, and conclude, "Let's face it. Sports are basically just testosterone contests." She may object to this by stating that she can beat a lot of men. Reply, "That proves my point. You obviously have a lot of testosterone."

No matter what her sport, you can ask, "How would the top women in your sport do against the top men?"

Conclude philosophically, "It's pathetic how people take their sports so seriously … it's just a game for Crissake. I mean, sports are fine for kids, but you're supposed to outgrow them sooner or later."

The Cryptic Comment

The best way to silence someone who fishes for compliments is to reply with a comment that will leave him wondering just what you meant.

Sometimes the best reply is simply the silent, expressive, almost exaggerated shrug; an insecure person will read all of his worries into that.

If your victim asks what you think of his new car, there are many answers to accompany that shrug that will leave him wondering:

"It's fine." ("Fine," in this context, always implies "barely adequate.")

"It'll do."

"One man's meat is another man's poison."

"Don't worry about it."

If it's an expensive car, shrug, "A fool and his money …"

Answering such a question with another question is equally obnoxious. Ask, "Why do you need my approval so badly?" This effectively turns his fishing expedition into yours.

If your victim asks for agreement with the "know what I mean?" formulation, reply, "If you say so."

If your victim argues his case for something, just shrug and reply, "I'm a skeptic by nature," as if your disbelief is a function of your personality rather than his weak case.

If he presses you, add, "Sorry, I'm a cynic."

Or if he asks you what you think of his performance at something, just reply, "Don't worry, I'm not a judgmental person," flattering yourself while at the same time implying that your victim should be judged very harshly. (Simply by making this comment, of course, you prove yourself very "judgmental.")

PART VII
Be Annoying

Make Him Feel Dumb

One of the most enjoyable activities you can have with your victim is to make him feel dumb.

One way to do this is to do the crossword puzzle at home first thing in the morning, then, when you see your victim, suggest the two of you do the crossword together. Find a fresh newspaper, then set the puzzle down in front of the two of you. He will feel increasingly dense as you scribble down the answers at a speed he could never hope to duplicate.

Suggest a game of Trivial Pursuit—after you have memorized the answers and stacked the deck ahead of time.

Watch the early edition of *Jeopardy* on TV, then challenge him to a game at the regular time.

Memorize a certain mathematical problem ahead of time. Then, when it is topical, say, "You know, I read the other day that the S&P 500 is expected to double every eleven years; it's at fourteen seventy-one right now, that means in thirty-three years it'll probably be around, let's see, eleven thousand, seven hundred and sixty-eight." His first thought will be, hmm, I couldn't possibly have done that calculation in my head that quickly.

After he proves his "stupidity" sometime, ask to see his hand. Then hold it in both of yours as if examining it, and put it down without a comment. He will ask you what you were doing. Reply, "I just wanted to see if you had an opposable thumb, that's all."

When a fact comes up that your victim is unaware of, ask, in a polite but slightly shocked tone, "You didn't know that?"

Eventually, you can condescend: when a fact arises that your victim *is* aware of, act surprised. Say, "Very good," as if to a seven-year-old.

You want to leave him feeling as if his brain is filled with cobwebs.

The Handshake

As every power player knows, the handshake is an art unto itself. When you greet your victim and shake his hand, don't extend your hand. Hold it low and perhaps three inches from your right hip. This strikes a very masculine, aggressive pose. It also compels your victim to lean forward slightly to reach your hand, and creates the impression—which will only sink in once he's done it—that he is bowing to you.

As his hand reaches yours, quickly envelop the tips of his fingers with your hand before your palms meet, and shake his fingers. This will make him the "limp fish" in the transaction, as if he is a woman who has offered her hand to be kissed. (How many of us have not experienced this feeling?) Pump his hand vigorously, increasing his limp fishiness. When the time comes to stop shaking, and he tries to withdraw, continue to grip his fingers firmly and keep pumping away, as if you are overjoyed to be seeing him again and literally don't want to lose touch. This will increase his haplessness. Utilize the muscles on the back of your arm to prevent him from pulling his hand up and away from your hip area. In fact, you should try to keep your right hand within six inches of your crotch, in such a manner that if you had an erection, the back of his hand would be rubbing it.

The coup de grace, if you can pull it off, comes when you take your left arm and put it around his neck, so that the back of his neck rests in the crook of your arm; he will instinctively pull his body away from yours, but your left arm should prevent disengagement. Touch your forehead to his (incline your head forward slightly, so that there is no risk of your lips touching.) At this point, you must growl something to the effect of, "It's really great to see you—we have to get together more often" in earthy, confident tones, so that your actions seem neither hostile nor homosexual. By this point, your victim will feel totally helpless, his hand trapped in yours and his head pulled right up against yours. Since you are being nominally friendly, he can't just push you away, so by now you have completely wet noodle-ized him. (A good shove is of course what you deserve at this point.)

Once the time has come when you absolutely must let go of his hand, rest your right arm on his left shoulder, and your left on his right, keep him relatively close. He will be left feeling very awkward and, unless he has the presence of mind to break your grasp and escape your embrace, as helpless as if you had him in a full nelson.

At this point, the only thing left to do would be to turn him around, pull down his pants, bend him over, and rape him.

The Sigh

There are no words quite so eloquently expressive of resigned disapproval as a weary sigh. This isn't just any old sigh, it's The Sigh: it must be deep, and the exhalation must be slow and very audible. You should also slowly shake your head as you let it out.

The most annoying thing about The Sigh is that it implies forbearance on your part, as if you're using your superhuman self-control to stifle the criticism that is on the tip of your tongue, when, in fact, The Sigh says it all—so the forbearance is false. It also implies that your victim's transgression is but the latest in a very long line.

If your victim makes a mistake, let out The Sigh.

If your victim repeats himself, let out The Sigh.

If your victim suggests an activity more to his liking than yours, let out The Sigh.

If your victim suggests an activity more to your liking than his, let it out.

The Sigh will always convey the same message: "You're sooooo tiresome."

It is sometimes said that if somebody makes you mad, you should count to ten before answering, otherwise you might say something in anger you will regret later on. If you want to anger your victim, count to ten out loud before answering. (This is The Sigh's first cousin.) The fact that you've counted out loud lets him know that he is trying your patience, and also proclaims that you are showing a great deal of self-control by counting instead of lashing out. But once again, your forbearance is false.

If your victim comments on The Sigh, profess innocence. Cry out, "All I was doing was breathing! Aren't I even allowed to do that anymore?"

The best thing about The Sigh is, if you make it deep enough, you can actually suck all the air out of the room—or at least make it feel that way to its other occupants.

Overshooting Your Victim's Observation

If your victim makes an observation you can't disagree with, render it weak instead. One way is to say, *"Ooooh yeaaaah,"* stretching each word out. This turns your victim's statement into an understatement.

Or, "You don't say," delivered very drily.

"To say the least!"

"You certainly have a penchant for stating the obvious."

"I first noticed that when I was six."

"Do you think the sun is going to rise in the east tomorrow too?"

"Well that's certainly going out on a limb."

If he says, "Susan is certainly an attractive girl," reply, "Attractive? She's unbelievably beautiful! I'd crawl across four miles of broken glass just to hold her hand!" This makes your victim's attraction seem like a wan, weak thing by comparison.

Avoid, "Amen, brother!" and "You said it," both of which indicate tacit approval as well as agreement. You want to register disapproval while nominally agreeing. Children accomplish this by saying, "Duh!" The adult version is a sarcastic "No kidding!"

Or just say, "Well, everybody can see that, the question is, where do we go from here?"

The outright declaration of war is, "No shit, Sherlock."

Praise His Rival

Nothing will drive your victim up the wall more than if you praise his bitter rival to the skies. This person can be a rival in any field: in business, in sports, academia, or love—the crucial thing is, he must both threaten and be despised by your victim.

So describe his rival as handsome (after all, this is a purely subjective judgment), as smart (a somewhat subjective judgment), as funny (subjective), and as a "great guy" (purely subjective). The implication, of course, is that the hated rival is superior in all these qualities to your victim.

Your victim will seethe, partly because he knows he must contain his jealousy or be deemed overly transparent.

To really twist the knife, describe your victim's rival as "charismatic." These days, the word "charisma" is misapplied to any number of dishonest politicians, self-involved actors, and childish sports figures. No amount of shallowness and egocentrism is enough to disqualify a candidate from having this quality. (Since journalists must create heroes where there are none, the c-word is invoked all too promiscuously.)

So apply the word to your victim's hated rival. The beauty of this is that "charisma," much like "leadership," is nebulous enough to be hard to refute. Go on and on about how other people really like him, how popular he is, and what "animal magnetism" he has (another quality that is hard to disprove).

In fact, go ahead and describe all sorts of other people as charismatic. Leave your victim with the impression that he is among the few without this intangible quality.

"You Need Medication"

If you follow the advice of this book, at some point your victim will become livid. After he has exploded in anger at you, look at him in shock and suggest, "You need medication," as if he is a wild animal that requires sedation, preferably with one of those hypodermic darts shot from a safe distance.

Observe, "You have a real problem with your temper, don't you," as if this is a condition that comes over him spontaneously (with no help from you). Suggest with a tone of great concern, "You should take an anger management course."

Say, "You seem to have violent tendencies. Do you get into fights often?"

Look at him as if he is just another laboratory rat confirming your theories, and say sagely, "People with such extreme self-control issues are usually sociopaths."

Ask, "Has anyone ever taken a restraining order out against you? Because I may have to get one." (This prospect is sure to send your victim into a towering rage, all the more so because he now has a tangible reason to repress it.)

Ask, "Do you beat your wife?" Or just assume the worst and say, "Your poor wife." (If you *are* his wife, and he has never hit you, claim, "I'm a battered wife.")

Once his blood is really boiling, say, "You better be careful or you're going to have a stroke."

Afterword

Nobody is ever at his most clear-headed while
in the middle of a heated argument. In fact, people
can often lose their tempers and let loose with
knee-jerk profanity, which only prove that they
can't deliver the kind of personalized insult
addressing their opponents' vulnerable points.
So make sure you always have some well-aimed
ammunition at hand. Bear in mind that absolutely
no one deserves to be attacked for any reason
other than his character. But noxious people are
vain too, so feel free to disparage an egocentrist's
appearance. If he is short, tall, skinny, or fat—if he
is human—you'll find some poisonous barbs here.
Sometimes the most effective way to insult is to
just give a left-handed compliment. We all know
oafs so incredibly ham-handed that they can't
help being insulting. Pretend to be one of these
numbskulls and your victim can only seethe quietly.
Calling attention to either a pathetically scanty or
remarkably tawdry sex life is another good way to
abase. Demeaning his career may be the cruelest
insult of all. Just remember, any weakness is fair
game if you enjoy deflating outsize egos.

978-0-595-48729-5
0-595-48729-7